EXTERMINATION CAMP TREBLINKA

BOOKS OF RELATED INTEREST

The Battle for Auschwitz
Emma Klein

Belsen in History and Memory
Jo Reilly, David Cesarani, Tony Kushner and Colin Richmond (eds)

Between Auschwitz and Jerusalem
Yosef Gorny

An Englishman in Auschwitz
Leon Greenman

From Dachau to Dunkirk
Fred Pelican

From Thessaloniki to Auschwitz and Back, 1926–1996:
Memoirs of a Survivor from Thessaloniki
Erika Myriam Kounio Amariglio

Hasag-Leipzig Labour Camp for Women: The Struggle for Survival,
told by the Women and their Poetry
Felicja Karay

I Was No. 20832 at Auschwitz
Eva Tichauer

A Life Sentence of Memories: Konin, Auschwitz and London
Issy Hahn

EXTERMINATION CAMP TREBLINKA

WITOLD CHROSTOWSKI

VALLENTINE MITCHELL
LONDON • PORTLAND, OR

First published in 2004 in Great Britain by
VALLENTINE MITCHELL
Crown House, 47 Chase Side, Southgate
London N14 5BP

and in the United States of America by
VALLENTINE MITCHELL
c/o ISBS Inc., 920 NE 58th Avenue, Suite 300
Portland, OR, 97213-3786

Website: www.vmbooks.com

British Library Cataloguing in Publication Data

Chrostowski, Witold
Extermination camp Treblinka
1. Treblinka (Concentration camp) – History 2. World War,
1939–1945 – Concentration camps – Poland – Treblinka
3. Holocaust, Jewish (1939–1945) – Poland
I. Title
940.5'3185384

ISBN 0-85303-456-7 (cloth)
ISBN 0-85303-457-5 (paper)

Library of Congress Cataloging-in-Publication Data

Chrostowski, Witold
Extermination camp Treblinka / Witold Chrostowski.
p. cm.
Includes bibliographical references.
ISBN 0-85303-456-7 (cloth) – ISBN 0-85303-457-5 (pbk.)
1. Treblinka (Concentration camp) 2. Holocaust, Jewish
(1939–1945) – Poland. I. Title.

D805.5.T74C57 2003
940.53'185384 – dc21
2003044573

Typeset in 10.5/12.5pt Zapf Calligraphica by Frank Cass Publishers
Printed in Great Britain by MPG Books Ltd, Bodmin, Cornwall

Contents

Acknowledgements

Many people contributed to this work. Special thanks go to:
My parents – for their patience.
My younger brother Grzes – for permanent and devoted support.
My Grandmother Leokadia.
Magdalena.
Raphael Scharff – who made it all possible and whose advice encouraged me to prepare an English version of this work.
Professor Marian Zgórniak – my tutor, whose patience and advice helped me on many occasions.
Professor Krzysztof Pilarczyk – who helped me a great deal, provided me with much helpful advice and supported me from the beginning.
Professor Piotr Kaczanowski – who put his trust in me.
Professor Wojciech Rojek – who helped me to deal with the Polish administration system.
My multinational friends and colleagues for being 'The Light in Darkness'.
The Department of History, Jagiellonian University, for co-financing the translation.
Dr Joachim Russek, for co-financing the translation.
Dr Manfred Burba – for kind permission to use the plan of Treblinka, map of Poland and two diagrams in my book.
Last but not least – Dr Maria Piotrowska, for the translation.

Introduction

The Treblinka extermination camp was the most notorious of all Nazi camps. During the 13 months of its existence 870,000 people were robbed and murdered in it.

The main task of this book is to show the structure and history of Treblinka II. The first chapter is an introduction to Operation Reinhard. It describes German preparations for the 'Final Solution' – from the T4 operation to the Wannsee conference. The author wanted to describe the history of euthanasia in Germany as a prologue to mass extermination of the European Jews, stressing the involvement of T4 members in Operation Reinhard.

The next two chapters detail the construction of the camp and personnel structure in Treblinka. Based on the evidence of witnesses and court documentation, Chapter 2 describes the beginnings of the camp – the place where it was built, its construction, and the people who participated in the operation.

Chapter 3 concerns the camp personnel – Germans, Ukrainians and Jewish prisoners. It reconstructs its structure, equipment, personnel duties, and the way the staff behaved. In the case of the Germans and Ukrainians, the author has included a list of the names of all those staff members who have been mentioned by witnesses. Details of the Jewish work kommandos, their 'colours' and duties, are also given. Additionally, the chapter contains a list of the names of the *kapos* and the so-called 'Jewish commanders'.

Chapter 4 is an attempt to describe the killing procedure used at Treblinka. It is based on testimonies from the relatives of witnesses and documentation from the trials of the German camp personnel. This chapter outlines the exact procedure of transport and the extermination of Jews as used in all Operation Reinhard camps. A separate section is devoted to the robbery of the victims – the way their belongings proceeded from the sorting square, through detailed selection to the railway wagons heading for the Reich. The author has tried to show how cruel and merciless the German killing machine was; before people had even reached the gas chambers, their belongings had already been fallen on by their killers and had begun to be sorted.

Chapter 5 is the true history of the camp Treblinka II, described almost day by day, in as much detail as possible: its social life, the development of the camp, relations between the staff and the prisoners, main events in the camp's life such as the arrival of the largest transports, desperate attempts at resistance and escape, and finally the system by which the bodies were burned.

The story of Treblinka II is of course full of terrible situations, cruel executions and tragic events, such as the typhus epidemic; however, it has some bright moments too – when people *in extremis* tried to help one another.

Chapter 6 details the preparations for the uprising that took place in Treblinka and the uprising itself described by its participants. It is the story of the underground Jewish organization in the camp, which tried to save as many lives as possible, and instigated the uprising. This story is a great exemplar of human solidarity against a common evil. The planning and execution of an uprising, in the terrible conditions prevailing in the camp, can only be described as an act of extreme bravery and courage. The chapter concludes with the history of the camp from the uprising until its liquidation in November 1943.

Chapter 7 summarizes the camp's story – from the beginning (spring 1942) until the very end (late autumn 1943). It tries to detail all the transports that arrived at Treblinka during that period, and attempts to arrive at a figure for the approximate number of people killed, using a method of counting developed especially for this work by the author. All statistics presented in this chapter are as accurate as possible. They are based on all published documentation and the accounts of witnesses. However, it is clear that it will never be possible to determine the exact number of Treblinka victims. The final part of Chapter 7 includes brief information about the main German characters who either took part in preparing Operation Reinhard or belonged to the staff of the Treblinka camp.

The book is supplemented by two annexes comprising short presentations of two other extermination camps – Belzec and Sobibor.

In his research for this work the author used various materials. The main sources for the history of Treblinka are the accounts of witnesses, such as the memoirs of Samuel Willenberg, Franciszek

Ząbecki, Jankiel Wiernik, Samuel Rajzman and many others. Material taken from the trials of Treblinka personnel were also extensively used.

In Poland, literature about German death camps is limited. During the communist period the topic of Nazi occupation was very popular and places such as Auschwitz and Treblinka served the government propaganda machine as the sites of martyrdom of the Polish nation. During that period authors like Grossman (1945), Łukaszewicz (1946) and Wojtczak (1975) tried to gather information about the camp and, using language typical for that time (e.g., 'german' instead of German – Grossman; Jews dying with the slogan 'Long live Stalin and the Red Army' on their lips – Łukaszewicz), show the history of Treblinka. A work by Ryszard Czarkowski (1989), which is still available at the Treblinka museum, exaggerates the number of victims.

On the other hand, during the communist period many memoirs of the survivors were published, mostly by ŻIH (Żydowski Instytut Historyczny – the Jewish Historic Institute, Warsaw). Those publications are very important. The memoirs of Willenberg, Rajzman, Krzepicki, Wiernik and Ząbecki had a great impact on research about Treblinka.

In western Europe, there is quite an extensive bibliography on Treblinka, to mention only the most important authors like Arad, Donat, Burba, Steiner and many others. Memoir literature is also quite sizeable. It contains books from both sides of the fence – Jewish prisoners who escaped from the camp during the uprising (Glazar) and interviews with German guards who served at Treblinka (Stangl, Suchomel, Franz).

The latest research indicates that during World War Two Poland lost 1,860,000 Jews. Their loss was a great tragedy not only for Polish culture but also for Polish society in general. With the loss of the Jews, Poland ultimately lost the multinational character that had been its treasure for centuries.

1 • German Preparations for the 'Final Solution' to the 'Jewish Problem'

They are dreaded and feared. Their justice and authority origi-nate with themselves.[1]

THE ORIGIN OF OPERATION REINHARD: OPERATION T4, EUTHANASIA OF THE MENTALLY ILL

In order to better understand the mechanism of Operation Reinhard it is necessary to trace the history of the T4 operation, as the 'Final Solution' is deeply rooted in the programme of euthanasia. In his book, *Mein Kampf*, Hitler repeatedly made it clear that the weak would have no place in his State:

> The stronger species will drive off the weaker one, because the desire to live in its ultimate form will break all funny shackles of the so-called 'humane individual', to make room for humanitarian nature to destroy what is weak and to offer room for the strong.[2]

On 14 July 1933, an act was passed concerning 'the preventive measures for giving birth to individuals with hereditary defects', which left the possibility of practising euthanasia open for Nazi doctors, and introduced a precedent for using law against practically any form of human life.

Hitler's personal physician, Dr Karl Brandt, at his trial before the American War Tribunal in August 1947, testified that in 1935 Hitler had a conversation with Dr Gerhard Wagner, the Head Physician of the Reich, in which he said that in the event of an outbreak of war, extermination of the mentally ill should be carried out. The Führer believed that the problem could be more easily and cleverly solved during the war, because 'an open protest, which could be expected from the Church, would not play such a major role during the war as it would under ordinary circumstances'.[3]

Dr Wagner, who had already focused on euthanasia in the past, prepared a special advertising film for the purpose of the project, which was entitled *Heritage*. In 1937 another film, called *Victims of the Past*, was shown. In addition other methods were used to influence public opinion, among which was an emphasis on what a drain the 'mentally ill' constituted to society. Here are some statistics from a set prepared by Adolf Boner and published in 1935:

> In one province of the Reich there are 4,000 mentally ill people … in state institutions, 4,500 in social care institutions, 1,600 in local institutions, 2,000 in homes for epileptics and 1,500 in charity homes. The state pays at least 10 million DM yearly for those institutions. How much is the yearly maintenance of one patient? The construction of a mental asylum costs 6 million DM. How many new apartments could be built for this amount if one costs 15,000 DM?[4]

The propaganda campaign lasted continuously until the end of 1938, when an event took place that confirmed Hitler's will concerning euthanasia. Hitler was approached with a written request by a certain Knaur, a father of a new-born mentally retarded child, for permission to end the child's life. Having consulted a group of physicians, the Führer agreed, and recommended that in future his office consider favourably each application of this kind. The problem of euthanasia resurfaced in summer 1939 when, during the preparations for the war with Poland, Hitler contacted Dr Brandt, Dr Leonard Conti (who then filled the position equivalent to that of the Minister of Health) and Philip Bouhler (chief of Hitler's office), and told them that a certain number of the mentally ill must be eliminated to clear hospital rooms.

Towards the end of October 1939, after the military campaign in Poland had ended, Hitler issued another order to be antedated 1 September 1939, whose contents read as follows:

> I command Reichsleiter Bouhler and doctor of medicine Brandt, and I make them responsible for extending personal authorization to appointed doctors to make decisions about using euthanasia with patients who are judged incurably ill to the best physicians' knowledge and expertise.[5]

Conti, as 'Bormann's man', was excluded from the programme.

Hitler's command was never issued officially; it was merely an internal order. After the war, the question of whether the document was not published in order to avoid objections from the public and the Church was answered by Victor Brack, Deputy Secretary in Hitler's office: 'I wish I had seen anyone in those days putting forward objections against a document signed by Adolf Hitler, regardless of the form of such a document.'[6]

Three legal bodies were appointed to carry out the project, namely the State Co-operative of Health and Care, the Foundation for Public Utility of Enterprise Health Care, and the Society of Public Utility for Transport of the Sick. The first of these dealt with seeking out the ill by distributing and then analysing questionnaires, the second organization financed the whole operation and prepared adequate death centres, the third one went about transporting the ill to those centres.

About 15 physicians were let in on the plans and their task was to make diagnoses. One of those doctors, Dr Fritz Mennecke, who was convicted during the trial of the employees of The Eichberg Centre, described the first meeting of the group of physicians with the supervisors of the operation:

> At the meeting, there were about ten to twelve other doctors apart from myself, whom I did not know. Doctors Hevelmann, Bohne and Brack announced that the national-socialist authorities of the country had issued acts, pursuant to which 'life unworthy of keeping' (literally 'life unworthy of living') may be put to an end. We, the gathered, were asked if we wanted to be medical experts. It was emphasized that the matter was strictly confidential; of top-secret national character. During the conference, Mr Brack read a letter whose contents I cannot recall exactly. However, I remember that the physicians engaged in the operation were to be treated with full impunity. Then the activities that were required of us doctors were discussed; that is, making diagnoses about the condition of patients from mental asylums. The other physicians apart from myself were middle-aged and as I learned later, there were some celebrities among those present. Because all of them gave their consent without any objections, I also agreed to be one of the experts.[7]

His supervisor, Reichsleiter Philip Bouhler, appointed Victor Brack the person responsible for conducting the entire operation on behalf of Hitler's office. There was a special Department II created for him, called 'Euthanasia'. The Führer instructed Bouhler that 'Hitler's office should by no means be linked with any activities in that domain'.[8] Since the organizers of the operation had their offices in one of the buildings of the Ministry of Internal Affairs in Berlin at no. 4, Tiergarten, the project received the codename T4.

During the period from 1940 to 1941, the following centres were adapted to the needs of the operation:

1. Grafeneck in Wirtemberg, started as the first centre and operated until the end of 1940. Headed by Dr Horst Schumann.

2. Brandenburg on the Havel, in operation from the end of 1940 until autumn 1941. Dr Irmfried Eberl was appointed the head of the centre.

3. Bernburg on the Saala, in operation from the end of 1940 until autumn 1941. Headed by Dr Heinrich Bunke.

4. Hadamar at Limburg, in operation from the end of 1940 until autumn 1941. Headed by Dr Berner.

5. Sonnenstein at Dresden, in operation until autumn 1941. Headed in turn by Dr Paul Nietsche and Dr Horst Schumann.

6. Hartheim at Linz, in operation from spring 1940 to autumn 1941. Headed by Dr Rudolf Lonauer.

A certain number of mentally ill people were killed outside the institutions. In Działdowo camp the sick were murdered in death trucks; that is, in mobile gas chambers located in trucks.[9] SS-Sonderkommando Lange was responsible for those actions.

The Central Security Office was approached to suggest an appropriate method of killing the ill; office 5 housed the Institute for Criminal and Technical Matters. Professor Albert Widmann, the head of the department of chemistry and physics at the Institute, proposed using carbon monoxide (CO) and promised to see that it was supplied to particular euthanasia centres. Moreover, in a report, he also suggested the use of other means, such as morphine, scopolamine, prussic acid, etc. For the purposes of the euthanasia operation for the mentally ill, small gas chambers capable of killing about ten to fifteen people at a time were quite sufficient.

The first gassing took place in Brandenburg in December 1939, in a bathroom-like gas chamber constructed by Christian Wirth[10] and Victor Brack. After four victims had entered the chamber, the door was hermetically sealed and a special pump turned on to pump carbon monoxide inside. After ten minutes all four were dead on the floor. The chamber was ventilated and then a special squad removed the bodies and cleaned the room. The whole event was observed by several invited guests including Brandt, Bouhler, Conti, a few other physicians, and the chemists Widmann and Becker.

The euthanasia operation lasted till August 1941. Because of the disruption caused by Operation Barbarossa (Hitler's invasion of Russia in 1941), and on account of frequent complaints from civilians living in the vicinity of the above-mentioned centres, Hitler verbally ordered Brandt to complete operation T4. Surprisingly, the killing of mentally ill and retarded children was continued until the end of war. It is impossible that such an operation could have been conducted without Hitler's permission; hence Jan Mikulski's hypothesis in his book (extensively quoted here), *Nazi Medicine in Service to the Third Reich*, that Brandt was ordered not to stop T4, but to restrict the operation and disguise it better.[11]

A consequence of this order was the closure of the majority of extermination centres, and the transfer of their staff to the Reich Office. These staff members now proved rather inconvenient for the system, because there was the danger that they would leak sensitive information about the programme to their families and friends.

In fact, at the beginning of spring 1941, Himmler had approached an SS physician, Dr Ernst Grawitz. The latter recommended to the Reichsführer a group of highly qualified technical staff from the euthanasia programme, who were temporarily unemployed. Christian Wirth, the above-mentioned police superintendent and a former director of the 'sanatorium' for the mentally ill in Hartheim, directed the group. These people were under the direct supervision of Hitler's office, even though their role in the T4 programme had ended. Thus, in view of the plans to carry out mass extermination of Jews in the East, SS-Oberführer Victor Brack, the supervisor of section II in Hitler's office, which was responsible for the T4 programme, received instructions to transfer his best people to the SS.

A group of 92 people was selected from among the medical staff of the euthanasia programme. The group included Wirth, Franz Stangl, Franz Suchomel, Otto Horn, Gustav Münzberger, Gustav Wagner and Kurt Franz; people with a sense of duty, highly experienced, of impeccable standing in the Party and characterized by complete devotion to the 'cause'. They also had equipment, because it had been sent by rail to Berlin after the T4 centres had been closed. From Berlin the equipment and installations necessary for the correct operation of gas chambers were sent to Lublin.

Reichsführer-SS Heinrich Himmler made Globocnik responsible for the efficient running of the whole operation. Hence, he also became the kommandant of the planned death camps. Himmler was to be his direct supervisor, which underscores the importance of creating an efficient extermination system for Jews as far as the German authorities were concerned.

On 31 June 1941, barely a week after the war with the USSR had started, Reinhard Heydrich received an order from Hermann Göring:

> To complement the task imposed on you with the order dated 24 January 1939, namely the solution to the Jewish problem by way of emigration or evacuation, I hereby command you to make all necessary administrative, material and content preparations for the general solution to the Jewish problem in the area of Europe under German domination. The preparations should be conducted with the participation of central authorities. Simultaneously, I recommend that the general plan of administrative, material and content measures indispensable for implementation of the 'Final Solution' to the Jewish problem be submitted to me.[12]

In connection with Göring's order, at the end of November 1941, there was a meeting in Eichmann's office in Berlin, which was attended by his proxies from the whole of occupied Europe, Höss[13] included. They informed their boss about preparations for the "Final Solution" in the territories under their control. Among the issues settled at the meeting were the problems of railway transport, timetables and prisoners' accommodation.

In the meantime Wirth's group was given a job to do; namely

the construction of the first experimental extermination centre in Chelm on the Ner. They were to create a centre modelled on the 'sanatoria' in Hartheim or Sonnenstein, with the difference that mobile gas chambers were to be used in the new location. These were called 'Rausch's trucks' after their constructor. Chelm was to be the destination for the sick from the region of the so-called 'Warta Country'. Wirth was to be responsible for the completion of all the works in the camp, and he was also a co-author of the design. The construction, or to be precise the adaptation, of a local palace existing onsite, was completed in November 1941. The centre in Chelm was the first structure of its kind on Polish soil.

Experience gathered during the inter-war programme of euthanasia for the mentally ill, was applied in the new centre. Efforts were also made to try and increase the number of victims. The subjects in those experiments were Jews from the Lodz ghetto, Gypsies, typhus victims and Russian political officers.

The extermination camp was located in an old manor house situated in a small park. The victims were taken under guard to a dressing room in the cellars. The guards were dressed in white gowns and pretended to be medical staff. The convicts were ordered to leave all their money and valuables, as well as clothes, to be disinfected, after which they went up naked in groups of 50 or 60 to a loading platform beneath a sign 'To the bathroom'. Here they were loaded on to the truck – a massive grey vehicle with a steel floor and walls. After the last victim had entered the truck, the door was closed tight and the driver, an SS-man from the Totenkopf watch troops, steered it into a forest in which a pit had been freshly dug. The driver left the vehicle's engine running, and at the touch of a button he started the system that pumped deadly fumes into the sealed truck. Death usually took its toll within five minutes; however, it sometimes happened that the truck was not sealed tight enough and the whole process lasted much longer. When the terrible screams stopped, the driver went up to the pit, opened the door and an SS man lifted up the back of the truck with a lever so that the corpses fell down into the pit like sand from a dumper. The bodies were further processed by Ukrainians and Jews, who pulled out gold teeth and took off rings. Meanwhile, the driver got back into his truck and returned for his next consignment of victims. Generally, in Chelm there were three vehicles marked 'Sonderwagen' – special vehicles in the inventory. Gassing took place from 7 am until dusk every day.

Death trucks were not efficient. There were cases of Jews breaking through the back door and escaping. Also, desertion was not
uncommon among the truck drivers. Theirs was not an easy job;
they had to sit in the front of the vehicle and wait for the people in
the back to die, listening to inhuman cries, desperate attempts to
open the door, scratching on the walls. This was bound to disturb
the psychological balance even of the most hardened and eager SS
men.

Experiences at Chelm prompted the decision to use permanent
gas chambers at the next three extermination centres. In these new
chambers, stronger poison gases would also be used to achieve a
more efficient result.

The prepared chambers were identical to the ones used in
mental asylums during operation T4. A specially trained SS man
supervised the running of the engines and the composition of the
fuel mix. However, not long after the extermination centres started
up it became evident that the solution was far from perfect; old
machinery broke down and the fuel was needed at the front.
Hence, an intensive search was carried out for a new method that
would be less costly and more reliable.

The problem found its own solution. The Tesch und Stebnow
corporation supplied Auschwitz with a gas called Zyklon B (crys-
tallized prussic acid), which was used to kill insects. One of the officers (Fritzsch, Höss's deputy) put forward the idea of trying this
gas on Soviet prisoners. The first experiments in this direction took
place in the basement of Block 11 at Auschwitz camp. Höss
recalled:

> Only a short, almost stifled cry and it was all over … I
> imagined this kind of death as painful suffocation. The
> bodies though did not have any traces of cramps …
> prussic acid paralyzes lungs; its effect, however, is so
> quick and strong that it does not cause any symptoms of
> suffocating as is the case with photic gas or cutting off
> oxygen.[14]

The tests with prussic acid proved so efficient that it was
decided that the concentration camps in the region of the 'Final
Solution' (Auschwitz, Majdanek) would receive bigger crematoria

and new, 'more efficient' gas chambers, in which Jews would be killed by means of Zyklon B.

The extermination centres of Operation Reinhard, at Wirth's order, were to be equipped with installations using petroleum as fuel. No firm official decisions were made at first about the number of people to be killed in this terrifying way; however, cautious estimates proposed that 10,000 to 20,000 human beings could be killed daily in each of the future death camps.

THE WANNSEE CONFERENCE

Should international Jews in Europe and beyond its boundaries again plunge nations into the next world war, the consequence would not be the bolshevism of the planet, meaning the victory of Jews, but the total annihilation of the Jewish race in Europe.[15]

On 20 January 1942, in the Berlin district of Wannsee, a meeting took place in one of the main buildings of the Central Security Office of the Third Reich, at 53/58 Am Grossen Wannsee Street. The date of the meeting had been announced a few weeks previously, and it was chaired by SS-Obergruppenführer Reinhard Heydrich, Chief of the RuSHA (Central Office for Race and Resettlement).[16]

For almost a year nearly all of the principal Third Reich offices had been engaged in preparations for the solution to the 'Jewish Problem' in Europe. Operations directed against 'the Jewish nation in the world' were actively planned by the Security Office, and also by Alfred Rosenberg's Ministry of the Eastern Territories, and Hans Frank, governor of the Government General (a Nazi-ruled territory in central and eastern Poland), who tried to prevent the Gestapo getting involved, and to solve the Jewish problem by himself.

Rosenberg did not consent to the idea of physical extermination of Jews, and he repeatedly expressed this in his orders. In May 1941 he issued an order in which he advocated strict repressive measures against Jews residing in the Baltic countries and eastern Poland. There was no mention in it of the physical extermination of those people; rather the problem was to be solved after the war.[17] For this reason, on 10 January 1942, Heydrich decided to write a short letter to Rosenberg, in which he asked him to change his order: 'The principles of our policy towards the Jewish issue were

formulated by the Central Security Office of the Third Reich …
They are to be implemented by SS-Obergruppenführer Eichmann[18]
… Under these circumstances I am forced to request a reprint of
your order.'[19]

Soon afterwards Rosenberg received a sheet of amendments
prepared by Eichmann, including this extract:

All measures undertaken in the occupied territories in
the east should be considered from the perspective of the
overall settlement of the Jewish issue in the whole of
Europe. That is why such actions which contribute to the
'Final Solution' of the Jewish problem, that is the elimination of Jews, should not be restrained in the occupied
territories in the east. It is especially in the occupied
eastern territories that all measures should be taken to
immediately solve the Jewish problem. For this reason
the local population should have no obstacles in their
actions against the Jews. Until appropriate measures are
taken in order to eliminate Jews, the local Jews ought to
be strictly isolated from the rest of the population. With
reference to all Jews there should be issued a prohibition
to move freely. Jews are to be transferred to ghettos.
Guarding the border between the ghetto and the outside
world is a police task. No economic considerations
should restrict the measures taken to eliminate Jews. All
Jewish property is to be registered and its removal or
transfer is to be prevented.[20]

As the whole operation was encountering increasing problems,
there was a need to convene a conference to discuss the controver-
sial issues and prepare a common approach to the solution to the
'problem' of approximately 11 million Jews in Europe.

Eichmann, a subordinate of Heydrich, was the initiator of the
meeting, and he also prepared the agenda and the list of participants. The invitees were asked to regard the meeting as obligatory,
owing to the 'extraordinary importance of the problem and the
necessity of establishing a common point of view'.[21]

Apart from Heydrich, the principal host, and the chief of the
secret police, SS-Obergruppenführer Müller,[22] the conference was
attended by the representatives of the highest political leaders and
ministers: Gauleiter Dr Meyer and Reichsamleiter Dr Leibbrandt,

who represented the Ministry of the Occupied Eastern Territories; Dr Stuckart, the Secretary of State in the Ministry of Internal Affairs; Neumann, the Secretary of State in the Ministry of Aviation; Dr Freisler, the Secretary of State in the Ministry of Justice of the Third Reich; Dr Bühler, the Deputy Secretary of State in the Governor General's Office; Dr Luther, the Deputy Secretary in the Ministry of Foreign Affairs; SS-Oberführer Klopfer, the representative of the Party Office; Ministerialdirektor Kritzinger, representing the Office of the Reich; SS-Gruppenführer Hoffmann from the RuSHA; and SS-Oberführer Dr Schongarth, the chief of the Gestapo and SD in the Government General. These were the secretaries and heads of departments of Göring, Himmler, Frick, Lammers, Bormann, Rosenberg, von Ribbentrop and Hans Frank, Governor General, maliciously called 'the king of Poles' behind the scenes.

Apart from 12 office workers there were two young SS officers: namely, recently promoted SS-Obersturmbannführer Adolf Eichmann and SS-Sturmbannführer Dr Rudolf Lange, chief of SS and police in the Latvia region and representative of the Central Security Office of the Reich at the Ministry of Eastern Territories, who had completed the extermination of the ghetto in Riga a few hours prior to the meeting. Due to that operation, and because of the need for Lange's participation, Heydrich postponed the conference twice. The young Sturmbannführer was an expert both in the subject of massive executions and in the use of gas-chamber trucks.

The conference opened with Heydrich's presentation, which recalled the order received from Göring on 31 June 1941 concerning the 'Final Solution'.

Heydrich reminded everyone that irrespective of geographical boundaries, the RuSHA was responsible for carrying out the extermination order, with other offices having a merely ancillary role in the project. Subsequently, he presented a short report on the ways of fighting Jews in Germany, recommending:

1. Removal of Jews from all spheres of social life in Germany.
2. Removal of Jews from the territory of the Reich.

In order for these efforts to bring measurable results the emigration of Jews from Germany should be intentionally accelerated, according to Heydrich. It is worth recalling that the Reich Central Office for Jewish Emigration had been established on Reichsmarshall

Hermann Göring's orders in January 1939. Heydrich, being the chief of the Central Security Office of the Reich, received the following tasks:

1. To make every possible effort to prepare for the increased emigration of the Jewish population.
2. To control the flow of emigration.
3. To accelerate the procedure in each individual case.

In brief, the goal was to clear German lands of Jews by means of 'legal procedures'. The plan had its advantages and disadvantages. It undoubtedly made the comparatively bloodless emigration of Jews from Germany possible; however, due to a flood of emigration petitions the emigration project caused complete chaos within a short period of time in the offices that dealt with emigration applications. Moreover, financial obstacles, the lack of an adequate transportation system, and limitations introduced by some countries on the entry of immigrants caused further problems for the 'emigration plan'. However, the state administration was forced to tolerate this state of affairs because, for the time being, there was no alternative plan.

In spite of the problems mentioned above, RuSHA data indicate that between 1933 and 1941 some 537,000 Jews left Germany, including:

- approximately 360,000 who were in the territory of Germany in 1933
- 147,000 who were in Austria before 15 March 1939
- approximately 30,000 who were in the Czech and Moravia Protectorate as of 15 March 1939

The project was financed either by the Jews themselves or by Jewish political organizations. In order to avoid leaving poor Jews behind in Germany a special tax called the emigration tax was introduced for well-to-do Jews, to cover the emigration expenses of those Jews who could not afford to leave the country.

Together with the exchange of German marks, a certain sum of money was to be presented by emigrants at the border. To avoid depleting the foreign currency reserve of the Bank of the Reich, it was agreed that foreign Jewish organizations would be responsible for coming up with the money for the emigrants who were in their hands. Up until 30 October 1941, US$ 9,500,000 in all was paid to

German Jews by such foreign organizations.

In May 1941, Heinrich Himmler, on Hitler's orders, halted further emigration of Jews from the territory of the Third Reich, due to the war situation and the newly created 'possibilities in the east'.

All these 'efforts' at solving the Jewish problem may have provided experience for the Hitler administration, but they proved to be effective on a local scale only. The only possible way to resolve the situation, in Heydrich's opinion, was the systematic and well-planned extermination of Jews living both on German soil and in the occupied territories.

Heydrich cited a few figures to illustrate 'the scope of the problem': five million Jews remained in the USSR; 2,284,000 in the Government General; 1,144,700 in the countries occupied in the west and north of Europe; and 742,800 in Hungary, Ireland, Great Britain, Switzerland, Spain, Turkey and Sweden. Heydrich's list included Estonia as the only *Judenrein* area – territory free from Jews. Approximately 11 million people were in mortal danger then, and 'the 'Final Solution'' was to be genocide on a scale previously unheard of in human history.

TABLE 1
JEWS IN EASTERN AND CENTRAL EUROPE 1920–31

Country	1920–25	1930–31
Poland	2,855,318 (10.5%)	3,113,933 (9.8%)
Czechoslovakia	354,342 (2.42%)	356,830 (2.42%)
Hungary	473,355 (5.9%)	444,567 (5.1%)
Romania	–	756,930 (4.2%)
Lithuania	157,527 (7.26%)	–
Latvia	96,675 (5.2%)	–
Estonia	4,566 (0.4%)	–

Source: Mendelsohn, E., *Zydzi Europy srodkowo-wschodniej w okresie miedzywojennym* (Warsaw: PWN, 1992).

Based on general censuses performed between 1920–25 and 1930–31. In some of the countries (Romania, Baltic states) it was done only once.

The main problem in any given country, according to Heydrich, was the difficulty in establishing who was of Jewish origin. This was especially true of Hungary and Romania where, based on RuSHA data, Jews could obtain documents certifying their citizenship of another country, albeit with much difficulty.

The USSR remained a unique territory in which, according to Heydrich, the influence of Jews on social life was particularly marked. Approximately five million Jews were citizens in the eastern part of this country, whereas in the Asiatic part they constituted a minority of a quarter of a million.

Heydrich explained that the next possibility could be the 'evacuation' of Jews to the east, and he mentioned 'the practical experience in the east', by which he meant the terrifying actions of the Einsatzgruppen[23] units in the territories conquered by the Germans in the USSR. Heydrich suggested that such actions 'will provide important feedback for planning the 'Final Solution''.

The new project proposed that Jews be moved to so-called 'temporary ghettos', as Eichmann recorded in his official notes, and subsequently transferred further east. The stronger individuals during this operation would form work groups employed in the construction of roads, canals, etc.

> Undoubtedly, a great number of them will be eliminated naturally due to exhaustion. Those who survive, and it will be a group of the toughest ones, will be subject to a *special procedure,*[24] otherwise they would constitute a group of naturally selected and most resilient individuals that could cause the rebirth of the Jewish race. In order to conduct the final solution to the problem, Europe is going to be searched from west to east. In the European countries within the domain of our influence an official appointed by the Security Police will co-operate with an adequate representative of the Ministry of Foreign Affairs.[25]

Initially, Heydrich proposed the displacement of Jews from the territory of Germany and the Protectorate of Czechia and Moravia owing to 'accommodation problems' in the area, as he put it. He also announced that Jews employed in arms factories at that time would not be 'evacuated', as had been demanded by Göring's secretary.

At Hitler's personal request in Terezin (Theresienstadt), in the territory of the Protectorate of Czechia and Moravia, a model ghetto was organized, which was intended to house Jews over 65 years of age from the prewar lands of the Reich, Austria and of the

Protectorate, as well as those who had received the Iron Cross of first category. On 31 October 1941, about 30 per cent of the 280,000 Jews residing in Germany and Austria fulfilled the above criteria. Terezin was to show the world the generous attitude of the leader of Greater Germany towards Jews. In fact, it was an ordinary place of slow extermination of old people who were fit neither for slave work nor 'evacuation'.

Heydrich noted that any wider deportation operations would depend on the progress of the army. He proposed that an expert from the Ministry of Foreign Affairs liaise with his counterpart in the RuSHA on this matter, irrespective of the method of conducting the 'Final Solution' in a given country.

In Slovakia and Croatia the 'problem' did not exist owing to the splendid co-operation between the two departments. In Romania the government had already appointed a Commissioner for Jewish Matters, whose task was to co-operate with the German security service. Since the Hungarian government was evading the issue, it was decided to force Hungarians to accept such an official from Germany. In connection with preparations for the deportation of Jews from Italy, Heydrich announced a meeting with the local chief of police. The conference participants did not believe they would encounter any problems in carrying out their programme in France.

The Vice-Secretary of State in the Ministry of Internal Affairs took the floor and stated that some countries, in Scandinavia for example, would face problems when the whole operation had been completed. On behalf of his supervisor he suggested that the deportation of Jews from those countries be postponed. This should not have a negative impact on the whole project, he said, because of the small number of Jews there. He also mentioned that the Ministry of Foreign Affairs did not envisage any problems of a similar nature in the countries of southeastern and western Europe.

SS-Gruppenführer Hoffmann declared that he intended to send an expert from the RuSHA to Hungary in order to obtain a clear picture of the situation there before any appropriate RuSHA office started a deportation operation. It was decided that the expert there would function as an assistant to the police attaché in Hungary. In connection with the plans for the "Final Solution", the Nuremberg Laws would settle the issue of so-called 'mixed marriages' and their offspring.

SS-Gruppenführer Hoffmann explained that sterilization would probably be widely used because people of mixed blood faced with a choice between 'evacuation' or sterilization would almost certainly choose the latter.

Secretary of State, Dr Stuckart, stated that implementing the presented system of solving the issue of mixed marriages would create endless administrative problems. Secondly, if biological heritage was not to be overlooked according to the above principles, it was evidently better to introduce obligatory sterilization. Legal dissolution of such marriages was to be the next administrative problem.

Dr Josef Bühler, the representative of the administration of the Government General, where the greatest number of Jews under German occupation resided also spoke. He informed the meeting that in the territory under the governor's rule, the 'Final Solution' had already started and he demanded that the process be speeded up because, as he proved, most of the Jews in the Government General were unable to perform any work. He also agreed with the opinion that the whole project should be co-ordinated by the RuSHA and assured the delegates that he fully supported 'the matter' on behalf of Hans Frank, Governor General.

In this way the final decision was made to exterminate Jews biologically. The idea as such was not new because Heydrich had mentioned it at the first Berlin conference, on 29 September 1939, which in fact was a briefing for the commanders of the Einsatzgruppen. At that time, though, Germans had no means of transporting Jews to the place of execution. It was only in January 1942, when the Hitler Reich ruled almost the whole of Europe, the idea of destroying the European Jews at last seemed feasible.

The last problem discussed at the meeting was the manner in which 11 million Jews should be exterminated. Adolf Eichmann, who had remained silent until then, took the floor, saying that for the previous two months, since 8 December 1941, a trial camp undertaking direct extermination had operated in Chelm on the Ner in Warthegau. There, people were being killed with exhaust gases in trucks which were the same as those used by Lange in Russia. Eichmann emphasized the usefulness of such camps, but he proposed to implement a different method of extermination because mobile gas chambers posed many problems for their crews.

Eichmann mentioned his visit to the Auschwitz camp in summer 1941. Rudolf Höss was the commanding officer there, and in May 1941 he was called to Berlin to have a personal conversation with Himmler, which was conducted without any witnesses. Höss, in his *Autobiography* quotes an interesting fragment of what the Reichsführer-SS communicated to him: '[the] Führer ordered the final settlement of the Jewish issue,' said Himmler:

> We, SS, are to carry out the order. The places of extermination situated in the east will not be adequate to the wide scope of the project ... Jews are eternal enemies of the German nation and must be exterminated. All Jews, whom we get a hold of, shall be exterminated with no exception during this war.[26]

Soon afterwards, Höss recounts, Eichmann had gone to Auschwitz. Höss described his guest's stay in the following way:

> Eichmann introduced me to the plans of the operation in particular countries. ... Eastern part of Upper Silesia and adjacent areas of the Government General, and subsequently, depending on the situation, Jews from Germany, Czechoslovakia, and finally from the west, namely France, Belgium and the Netherlands ... Consequently we discussed the way of conducting extermination. Only gas could be taken into account because extermination of such huge human masses, which we expected would be totally impossible with the use of gunfire, and because of women and children, would burden the SS officers at work too much. Eichmann acquainted me with the method of killing by using exhaust gases in trucks, as has already been practiced in the east. However, it could not be implemented for mass transports that we would expect in Auschwitz. Killing with carbon monoxide in showers, as was done with the mentally ill in some localities in the Reich[27] would require too many buildings to use and also providing gas for so many people might be problematic ... Eichmann wished to find the kind of gas that could be easily produced and whose use would not require any special equipment ... Eichmann was not able

to give me the exact starting date of the operation, because it was still at a preparatory stage and Reichsführer SS did not issue an order then.[28]

Presenting his argument, Eichmann talked about the role of concentration camps in the planned extermination operation. For him, a network of effective death factories was the foundation of the whole plan. Eichmann had gained experience in the physical extermination of Jews in Russia by Einsatzgruppen units during the first year of the war, but he decided that the tactics should be changed. The personnel from those units quickly became depraved; participating in such bloodbaths caused irrevocable damage to the soldiers' psyche. Höss recalls, 'Suicide among Einsatzgruppen soldiers became very frequent. They were not able to cope with constant wallowing in blood. A few went mad. The majority of participating members of the operational force lived on alcohol while performing their terrible job.'[29]

Dr Lange followed Eichmann with a short report on various methods of exterminating Jews in the east. He expressed the same opinion as the preceding speaker concerning the necessity of using permanent centres of extermination, showing difficulties that the operation was faced with in the USSR. The execution of Jews was contributing to the increase of resistance and determination of the local population, he pointed out, which in turn was leading to a rapid increase in the number of guerrillas. Moreover, he complained that some Wehrmacht commanders made it difficult for the units of 'operational groups' to conduct their activities, and he requested a clear division of competence between Einsatzgruppen and forward military units of the German Army.

Hans Frank's representative expressed his supervisor's opinion that they should start the process of transporting to extermination centres both Jews from the ghettos of the General Government and those inhabiting the area of the former Polish State that was beyond the jurisdiction of the governor. Bühler explained that there should be no problems with organizing transport owing to the military actions. Moreover, because of its geographical location, Poland was precisely in the middle of German possessions acquired during the war, which additionally shortened all transportation routes. Everybody present at the meeting was aware that Poland was the country with the biggest Jewish population of all.

Bühler, concluding the speech, recalled the traditional Polish anti-Semitism, which could be exploited for the purposes of their project. He argued that Poles had no reason to object to the extermination of Jews, and that they might even co-operate with German units in the realization of the project.

The delegates unanimously agreed that the extermination operation would be headed by an institution created by Heydrich and directed by him. Adolf Eichmann, Heydrich's subordinate, was granted full authority to organize death transports for Jews all over Europe. All Reich offices confirmed their support for him. All 'emigration' methods were ultimately given up in favour of biological elimination. Eichmann and his people were to search Europe, gather Jews together, and send them to the place of extermination. Permanent centres would be established in order to 'modernize' the whole operation, and their only goal would be to murder as many people as possible. Finally, it was decided where such death factories would be located; and Poland, as judged by the participants of the conference, seemed to be the perfect place for these terrifying plans. Only one task remained: namely the preparation and construction of appropriate centres of mass destruction.

In connection with the planned Operation Reinhard, the majority of T4 personnel were transferred to Lublin. On Hitler's personal order, an additional page, red in colour, was inserted into their soldier's payment books and signed by the OKW (Oberkommando der Wehrmacht),[30] on which there was an instruction not to employ them in any form at the front. In that way the risk of any of them being captured by the Russians would be minimized. They were in possession of knowledge that could be a threat to the internal stability of the Third Reich.

Since Himmler had not allocated any extra manpower for conducting the whole operation, Globocnik had at his disposal just 92 former T4 employees to perform the gigantic task of resettling and sending to death two million Jews. In the Lublin district, all SS units and police were under his control. These included field security police posts (SiPo), police orderly units (OrPo) and military police. Of all these units, only three police battalions numbering about 1,500 people were prepared for this kind of operation.

Under the circumstances, two additional formations were to be assigned, namely the so-called 'Special Department' (Sonderdienst), which comprised small units of ethnic Germans living in

Poland before the outbreak of war, and also staff from the prisoner-of-war camp for Red Army soldiers in Trawniki. With Himmler's personal consent, Globocnik could start recruitment among citizens of the Soviet Union held in prison camps. This recruitment was carried out on the basis of anti-Semitic and anti-communist convictions of candidates, thus giving preference to residents of the former Baltic republics, and Ukrainians. The candidates were presented with a proposal of co-operation: the ability to leave the camp, decent working conditions and a promise that they would not be sent to the Eastern Front. Because of the intolerable conditions in the prison camps, there were very few cases of refusal. The enlisted were transferred to the Trawniki camp, which was transformed into an educational post. There they were divided into national groups and instructed by SS officers. Karl Streibel was appointed the person responsible for the efficient functioning of the recruitment and educational system.

Globocnik chose SS-Hauptsturmführer Hermann Höfle to be responsible for the group of former T4 employees. SS-Obersturmführer Helmuth Pohl became his assistant and Pohl was also made responsible for receiving transports. Christian Wirth, SS-Obersturmführer, took the post of technical inspector of extermination camps. In effect, Wirth became the inspector-general of all extermination camps, with responsibility for the efficient running of the whole operation. Members of his staff were sworn to secrecy. Höfle spoke personally to each of the candidates and then gave him the following declaration to sign:

> I was precisely instructed and informed by SS-Hauptsturmführer Höfle, the commander of the General Department of Operation Reinhard at the SS and Police Commander headquarters for Lublin District, that:
>
> - under no circumstances am I allowed to pass any information, either written or oral, to anyone outside the limited number of Operation Reinhard employees, about the progress, procedures or accidents during the evacuation of Jews
> - The process of the evacuation of Jews is a project conducted within 'top-secret Reich documentation' and is subject to censorship rules Versh V

- Taking photographs in Operation Reinhard camps is absolutely prohibited

I declare that I am acquainted with the above regulations and am aware of the responsibility resting on me in connection with the given task. I promise to fulfill them to the best of my abilities. I am aware that the order to keep the above information secret will be binding also after the service is finished.[31]

Special 'clearing troops' composed of SS forces, police and Ukrainian auxiliary units were to watch over the process of throwing the Jews out of their ghettos. Three SS officers were made responsible for the troops: namely, SS-Hauptsturmführers Georg Michalsen, Kurt Claasen and Ernst Lerch.

All stolen property, both in empty ghettos and in death camps, was to be gathered and sorted out, then taken to the Reich or directly to Lublin. Georg Wippern was to supervise and co-ordinate this action.

At the beginning of October 1941, construction of the first extermination centre in Belzec, to the southeast of Tomaszow Lubelski in the Zamojskie region, began. Since no installations of this type had existed in Germany before, the centre was considered an experiment. Work was supervised by SS-Oberscharführer Josef Oberhauser. After the arrival of Christian Wirth, Oberhauser was appointed the deputy kommandant of the camp. Belzec became the training ground for Operation Reinhard. This was where the methods of psychological influence on the victims were worked out, which were later used in Treblinka and Sobibor. This was also the place where the first experiments with the new type of gas chambers using fuel gas for killing people were carried out.

Experience gained at Belzec was used at the construction of the next extermination centre in Sobibor, a small village located to the southeast of Wlodawa, which came into being in March 1942. The last camp of this type, Treblinka, was constructed after camp Sobibor had been designed.

Both Treblinka and Sobibor were erected by a special group managed by two engineers: SS-Hauptsturmführer Richard Thomalla from SS Zentralbauleitung (the Central Construction Office of the SS), who replaced Oberhauser, and construction supervisor Moser from Berlin.

According to Heydrich and Himmler, permanent extermination centres were designed to play the key role in the planned operation. Camp personnel were to continue their terrifying job until they had accomplished the total annihilation of the Jewish nation.

NOTES

1. Habakkuk 1:7.
2. A. Hitler, *Mein Kampf* (Berlin, 1935) p. 145; quoted by J. Mikulski *Medycyna hitlerowska w służbie III Rzeszy* (Warszawa: PWN, 1981), pp. 35–6.
3. A. Mitscherlich and F. Mielke, *Nieludzka Medycyna* (Warsaw: Państwowy Zakład Wydawnictw Lekarskich, 1963), p. 185.
4. Exercises from the collection entitled *Mathematic im Dienste der nationalpolitischen Erzehung*; quoted by J. Mikulski *Medycyna hitlerowska* pp. 36–7.
5. See Mitscherlich and Mielke, *Nieludzka Medycyna*, p. 186.
6. See J. Mikulski, *Medycyna hitlerowska*, p.41.
7. Mitscherlich and Mielke, *Nieludzka Medycyna*, pp. 186–7.
8. P. Padfield, *Himmler, Reichsführer S*, Vol. 2 (Warsaw: Interart, 1997), p. 13.
9. The trucks were supplied by a private company, Gaubschat Fahrenwerke GmbH, from Berlin. They were converted from military ambulances – a 7.5-ton 'Saurer' measuring 5.8 m in length, 2.5 m in width and 1.7 m in height, and a smaller 3.5-ton 'Opel Blitz'. Some of them had the sign of Red Cross on their sides. See Th. Blatt, *Sobibor: The Forgotten Revolt* (Seattle: HEP, 1998).
10. Before World War Two, Christian Wirth was a criminal police superintendent in Stuttgart; while supervising the prison there, he gained notoriety for his idea of giving poisoned food to the prisoners. Wirth, called by his colleagues 'wild Chrystian', is remembered by his coworkers as a mentally unbalanced person who was incapable of higher human emotions. The above-mentioned gas chamber was constructed and then improved by him and Brack in a deserted prison at Brandenburg. He created the whole system of gassing there, which was subsequently used in all centres of operation T4 and Operation Reinhard.
11. Mikulski, *Medycyna hitlerowska*, pp. 47–9.
12. It was the famous order no. 'PS 710'; the first document in which the term "Final Solution" was used. A copy of the order was attached to each invitation sent to participants in the conference in Wansee; Mikulski, *Medycyna hitlerowska*, p. 52.
13. R.F. Höss, *Autobiography* (Warsaw: Wydawnictwo Prawnicze, 1989), p.188.
14. Ibid., p. 144.
15. Fragment of Adolf Hitler's speech in the Reichstag on 30 January 1939.
16. In German: *Reichssicherheitshauptamt* – the Central Security Office of the Third Reich.
17. A passage of the order, quoted by J. Heydecker and J. Leeb in, *The Third Reich from the Perspective of Nuremberg* (Warsaw: Książka i Wiedza, 1979), p. 467, and Lord Russell of Liverpool, *Eichmann's Trial* (Warsaw: Czytelnik, 1966), p. 52: 'A definite solution to the Jewish problem will be creating ghettos after Jews are eliminated from all public places … The Jewish problem in Europe will be generally solved after the war.'
18. Adolf Eichmann, born on 19 March 1906 in Solingen, NSDAP (Nazi party) member no. 899895; SS no. 45326. Highest rank: SS-Obersturmführer. Director of the 'Jewish' Department IV B4 at Office IV / Gestapo / RSHA.
19. Lord Russell of Liverpool, *Eichmann's Trial*, p.53.
20. Ibid., p. 56.
21. Ibid., p. 57.
22. Heinrich Müller, born 28 April 1900, NSDAP member no. 4583199 and SS no. 107043.

Distinguished with the award of the Ring and Sword badge of the SS. Highest rank: SS-Gruppenführer. Chief of the infamous Office IV of the RuSHA.
23. Einsatzgruppen, i.e. operation groups, were special Security Police and Services units, divided into the so-called 'Einsatzkommandos', operating in the rear of the German Army with the task of isolating or liquidating so-called 'unwelcome elements', i.e. political officers, police and customs officers, Jews, outstanding representatives of the community, prominent figures in the political and cultural spheres, artists and the intelligentsia. These units appeared for the first time after the annexation of Austria, then they operated in Czechoslovakia, in Poland (where the participants in the Silesia and Great Poland uprisings were murdered) and in the USSR, where four Einsatzgruppen denoted by the letters A to D shot approximately 20,000 people daily. According to the findings of the American Military Tribunal in Nuremberg, the activities of the 'operation groups' accounted ultimately for over two million human beings, including men, women, and children. Fourteen out of the 22 kommandants of the Einsatzgruppen and Einsatzkommandos were sentenced to death by the verdict of that Tribunal.
24. It is worth noting here that during the conference, there was not a single contribution indicating the possibility of solving the Jewish problem by biological extermination. Adolf Eichmann's notes written during the meeting provide interesting data to support this thesis. Words like 'deportation', 'resettlement', etc., in the Nazi reports and in such official notes as Eichmann's, meant 'shooting', 'gassing' or 'transporting to death centres'. In this particular case the euphemism *Sonderbehaldung* is of a similar nature. When asked by an Israeli officer during the hearing after the war 'What does it mean "to undergo a special procedur"?' Eichmann answered, 'Killed. Killed without any doubt.' Quoted by P. Padfield, *Himmler: SS Reichsführer, T.II*, p. 164.
25. See Lord Russell of Liverpool, *Eichmann's Trial*, pp. 57–8.
26. Höss, *Autobiography*, p. 186.
27. Operation T4.
28. Höss, *Autobiography*, pp. 186–7.
29. Ibid., p. 145.
30. Franz Suchomel, who was one of the staff at Treblinka, mentions this in an interview given to Gitta Sereny and quoted in her book, *Into that Darkness: From Mercy Killing to Mass Murder* (London: Penguin, 1998).
31. A. Rückerl, *NS-Vernichtungslager in Spiegel deutscher Strafprozesse, DTV Dokumente* (München, 1977), pp. 125–6.

2 • *Construction of the Treblinka Extermination Centre*

Behold, he goes up like clouds,
And his chariots like the whirlwind;
His horses are swifter than eagles.
Woe to us, for we are ruined![1]

TOPOGRAPHY OF THE TREBLINKA II CENTRE

Driving a car along the road paved with uneven flags rein-forced with concrete from the direction of Treblinka village towards Malkinia, it is hard to shake off the feeling of depression brought on by the surroundings. Both sides of the road are heavily forested with pine trees, and on the right-hand side there is an embankment of the railway, unused for almost 60 years, which is overgrown with grass and prickly thistle. Not a sound can be heard when you stop. Hardly any tourists visit the place.

It is the middle of summer but not a bird can be heard nearby. In the vicinity, there are many railway lines' crossings; it is exactly here, if you check on the map, where the railroads to Warsaw, Bialystok, Siedlce and Lomza intersect. During the war there was only one paved road in the area, the one leading among the trees towards the sandpit four kilometres away, which was built by prisoners of the labour camp Treblinka I.[2]

Here, on sandy barren soil about 1.5 kilometres from that infamous labour camp, the conditions for building a new extermination centre were perfect. The maze of railroads linking important centres made it particularly convenient, and the dense pine forests and remoteness of the sandy locality seemed to the Germans ideal for keeping their operations secret. An additional advantage of the place was the vicinity of the labour camp, which guaranteed the availability of a cheap workforce to be used for constructing the centre, as well as for maintaining it once built. Workers from Treblinka I, having completed their jobs, could also easily be got rid

24

of so that news of what went on in the forest would not reach the outside world. The Treblinka extermination centre was intended to receive all transports from the Warsaw and Bialystok ghettos; and the relative closeness of the two cities made it possible to limit the time between the loading of transports on carriages at the station and their unloading at the death camp to an hour and a half.

CONSTRUCTION PLANS AND THEIR IMPLEMENTATION

Construction of the extermination camp in Treblinka started at the beginning of April 1942. A few SS men came to the village of Poniatowo, and after inspecting the locality they earmarked land with a total area of about 13 hectares, located at the border between Poniatowo and Wolka Okraglik. A few weeks later, construction materials such as pipes, sanitary installation parts, cement and boards started to be brought to the site by trucks. Germans connected a telephone from the site to the post office. A road was built through the forest to the camp site.

Obersturmführer Richard Thomalla, who had previously fulfilled the same function at the Sobibor camp, supervised the work on behalf of the SS.[3] The workers who found themselves under his command were primarily Jews brought there by trucks from the neighbouring villages (Wegrow and Stoczek Wegrowski), and also prisoners – mostly Poles from the nearby labour camp Treblinka I – who had been selected for this purpose by its kommandant, Teodor van Euppen.[4]

The office of the commissioner of the Warsaw ghetto, SS-Untersturmführer Heinz Auerswald, supplied the construction materials.[5] The workers also used local supplies – wood (from tree felling), sand, and gravel from the nearby pit. A witness, Lucjan Puchala,[6] recalled:

> Initially we did not know the purpose of building the branch track, and it was only at the end of the job that I found out from the conversations among Germans that the track was to lead to a camp for Jews. The work took two weeks, and it was completed on 15 June 1942. Parallel to the construction of the track, earthworks continued. The works were supervised by a German, an SS captain.

At the beginning, Polish workers from the labour camp, which had already been operating in Treblinka, were used as the workforce. Subsequently, Jews from Wegrow and Stoczek Wegrowski started to be brought in by trucks. There were 2–3 trucks full of Jews that were daily brought in to the camp. The SS-men and Ukrainians supervising the work killed a few dozen people from those brought in to work every day. So that when I looked from the place where I worked to the place where the Jews worked, the field was covered with corpses. The imported workers were used to dig deep ditches and to build various barracks. In particular, I know that a building was built of bricks and concrete, which, as I learned later, contained people-extermination chambers.[7]

It was established that about 400 prisoners carried out the works. At the beginning of July, three more brigades of workers were brought in.

The layout and the area of the camp were almost identical to the one at Sobibor. On 14 hectares of sandy infertile land, in the very middle of a pine forest, wooden barracks were hastily built, a concrete ramp for unloading was constructed, the area of the future extermination camp was fenced with a wall made of barbed wire and thickly woven with pine twigs, and watch towers were erected. The whole process took about two months.

Where the branch line reached the camp, another ramp for unloading was built, with the capacity to handle 20 railway wagons plus the steam engine.

This area was fenced off from the rest of the camp, dividing the whole into two parts. At first the area was carefully guarded by SS men, and then, after the watch towers had been erected, by the Ukrainians. When the construction of the branch line was finished, wagons arrived loaded with barbed wire, anti-tank barriers, boards and building materials for the barracks. Finally a huge excavator arrived, of the type used for digging foundations. In the other part of the building several deep pits, each about 30 m long, were dug. This area of the camp was fenced with anti-tank barriers. Building materials were brought not only from Warsaw but also from Sokolow Podlaski and Kosow Lacki. Jewish communities supplied building materials as well as whole sets of tableware for the administrative personnel of the camp. A dedicated power station was also constructed in the camp.

During the construction work, Germans and Ukrainians brutally killed many of the Jewish workers. Jan Sulkowski[8] remembers:

> Germans killed Jews at work by shooting them or beating them to death with sticks. I saw two such cases, in which SS men, during the grubbing-out jobs, forced Jews to walk under the falling tree by which they were crushed. In both cases several (two, three or four) Jews were killed. It also happened that SS men would often rush into the barracks where, drunk or sober, they went on shooting at the Jews who were inside.[9]

There was not a single survivor among the Jews who worked on the construction of Treblinka II.

The camp was to be divided into two major parts and four smaller ones. The first one, which will subsequently be referred to as camp no. 1, was split into three smaller parts separated by walls of barbed wire thickly woven with pine twigs. The first section contained specially prepared buildings fitted out with items such as cash desks, semaphores, points, and a clock whose hands never moved, together with a concrete loading ramp, which together were intended to look like a small train station. This complex was in fact a barracks for storing the sorted belongings of the people who would be murdered at the camp. A branch line led off in a southerly direction; after a few dozen metres it disappeared somewhere behind a wall of barbed wire. This structure was always carefully covered with fresh pine twigs.

Close behind the station barracks, there was a sizeable square (Sortierungsplatz), on which a special Jewish kommando sorted out things brought by the people transported to the camp. Every single piece of clothing had to be carefully searched (for hidden jewellery) and folded neatly in a separate pile. Shoes were tied with shoelaces, and coats, suits, dresses, children's clothes, etc., were placed in separate piles.

In the eastern part of the square, where clothes were sorted out, there was a latrine surrounded by barbed wire. At the beginning, due to permanent problems with water and sewage, this single latrine could only be used by each prisoner for one minute. Soon afterwards another one was built on the assembly square. The time limit for using both latrines was controlled by a special *Szajskommando*.[10]

The southeastern corner of the square, where things were sorted out, was occupied by an 'infirmary' measuring thirty by six by two metres, and a pit into which bodies of those who did not survive the journey were dropped. The 'infirmary' was in fact a sham medical station, in which old, infirm and 'troublesome' people from the transport were shot. It was surrounded by a fence, two to three metres high, painted white. The victim was led clandestinely out from among the newcomers and taken to the sorting square so that the others would not witness what was about to happen. Two SS men[11] who worked in the infirmary wore white doctors' uniforms and Red Cross bands on their left arms. On entering the infirmary, the victim saw a vision of hell. Behind the fence, at a distance of two or three metres, there was a big pit in the ground containing half-burnt bodies. Here and there a fire smouldered. At the edge of the pit the victim was seated on a bench facing the burning grave. Then an SS man shot the victim in the head or neck, and pushed him/her into the pit. When the right number of bodies was collected in the pit, two Jews from the work kommando collected the corpses and set fire to them. It was also their duty to keep the fire burning. Executioners usually did not aim very precisely, so the bullet did not always cause immediate death; thus it happened that a still-conscious victim was sometimes burnt alive.

Beside the infirmary, there was also a pit for corpses from transports. Similarly, when the right number of bodies was collected in the pit, wood was thrown in, which Jews had to place in between the corpses. Petrol was poured over the bodies and they were then set on fire.

There was only one entrance for the newcomers from the ramp to the camp, in front of which lay a square for the selection of victims. Here their luggage was taken before transfer to the Sortierungsplatz, and here the young and healthy were selected for work kommandos, whereas the sick, infirm and 'exceedingly suspicious' were led to the infirmary.

Behind the entrance there were two barracks situated on opposite sides of the road, and a noticeboard with instructions for those who were being led to death. The barracks on the right-hand side (from the entrance) was used as an undressing room for men (although in fact men always undressed outside regardless of the season); the one on the left-hand side was meant for women. In the female barracks there was also a cash desk at which all valuables were to be placed in deposit, and hairdressers' stands close to the exit. The exit was located in the eastern wall of the barracks. Immediately in front of it there was a path, about 100 or 120 metres long and two metres wide, which was paved with white gravel and decorated with flowers. It was surrounded by barbed wire woven with fresh pine twigs, and it led up to gas chambers. Jewish workers called it 'The Pipe', whereas Germans gave it the name of *Himmfehlstrasse* – 'The Road to Heaven'. Contrary to popular opinion, the road did not lead through the forest, or even along its edge, but it was built on half-sandy soil about ten metres away from the nearest trees.

To the north of the dressing room for women, separated by a wall of barbed wire thickly woven with pine twigs, there was a 'camp for the living', which meant Jewish workers' quarters together with several workshops. That whole sub-camp, excluding the above-mentioned wall, was fenced with barbed wire, but it was not camouflaged so that the victims walking to their final destination could be 'reassured' that Treblinka II was not an extermination centre but just a small labour camp. The whole southern section was taken up by an assembly square (Appelplatz). To the north there were barracks for Jewish workers, a separate barracks for the so-called 'golden Jews', barracks for women, for carpenters, dressmakers, shoemakers, *kapos*, a place for the sick, a laundry room, a kitchen, sleeping quarters and a latrine.

To the north, beyond the area of the camp for 'the living', behind a wall of barbed wire, there were stables; and a dozen metres to the west, just by the entrance to the camp for Jewish workers, there were two buildings built during the late period of the centre, namely a textile workshop and a bakery.

A road leading through the area of 'the living quarters' up to the Treblinka–Malkinia crossroads was called Kurt-Seidel Strasse after a German officer who supervised the construction work. On the right-hand side of the road was located the Jewish workers' camp already mentioned, and a little nearer to the main gate of the centre, on the left-hand side of the road, there were SS barracks and their canteen. The building was divided into two parts and in between them there were two smaller sections, which shared walls with the main building. The first one housed showers; the second weapons and ammunition.

Opposite the SS barracks, on the other side of Kurt-Seidel Strasse, there was a barracks for young women who worked as servants in the camp, divided into two parts, one for Poles and the other for the Ukrainians.

A little further on, on the same side of the road, there was a building in which a dentist and a barber worked for the Germans. The same building also housed a sick room and a cellar adapted to serve as a shelter in case of air raids. Here, walking from the camp you could turn right or go straight ahead to reach the main gate. In both cases you had to pass by the quarters of the camp komman-dant, which were located right by the gate, at the corner of the road. It was the last (or first) building in front of the camp gate.

Following the road to the right, you could see a strange phenomenon on the right-hand side: namely, a small zoo built in the spring of 1943. On the other side of the road there was a cellar whose function is unknown. The road ended with the Ukrainian guards' quarters, called 'the barracks of Max Bialy' to honour the SS man who was killed by a prisoner sentenced to death.[12] It was a complex of five buildings housing the Ukrainians' sleeping room, a doctor's office, a barber, a kitchen, a canteen, and the so-called 'day room' (probably a common room). Behind the guards' buildings, within a distance of a few dozen metres, there were two cellars for storing potatoes, and behind those again, at the edge of the forest there was a small exercise ground for the Ukrainians.

The second part of the centre, subsequently called camp no. 2, occupied only one-sixth of the total area of the centre and was situated in its southeastern corner. Called the 'Totenlager' by the Germans, it was the true death camp. There were only two roads leading to the centre: one of them at the edge of the forest was meant for guards and personnel; the other one surrounded by walls of barbed wire woven with pine twigs was the above-mentioned road for the victims; the road of no return. In order to increase camp security and improve camouflage, two earth embankments were made – one from the east to hide collective graves, and one from the west to hide gas chambers. German workers dug both of them. Christian Wirth was the initiator and the designer. The contractors were a Leipzig company called

Schoenbronn, and a Warsaw branch of the company Schmidt und Münstermann.[13]

The building which housed first three gas chambers was built in the middle of the camp, approximately 50 metres from the end of the road for the victims. The chambers were not very big, each about five by five metres, and similar to those used in Belzec or Sobibor at that time. Together they were capable of killing a maximum of about 600 people at a time. The position of the building was not well thought out, because the presence of huge collective graves immediately to the left could cause panic among future victims.

A witness, Jan Sulkowski, who was one of the bricklayers working on its construction, described the building with the gas chambers:

> SS men said it was to be a bath. Only later on, when the building was almost completed, I realized that it was to be a gas chamber. What was indicative of it was a special door of thick steel insulated with rubber, twisted with a bolt and placed in an iron frame; and also the fact that in one of the building compartments there was put an engine, from which three iron pipes led through the roof to the three remaining parts of the building. … A specialist from Berlin came to put tiles inside and he told me that he had already built such a chamber elsewhere.[14]

Behind the building housing the gas chambers, within a distance of approximately 10–15 metres, there were barracks for the so-called 'Totenjuden',[15] meaning a work brigade working for the death camp. The barracks were surrounded with barbed wire and they stood close by the southern wall of the camp. Inside there were rooms for women, a doctor's office, *kapo* barracks, showers, a latrine and a barracks for men and kitchens. A laundry stood outside.

In the middle of the death camp there was a watch tower, which was erected in the spring of 1943; and a well below. About 15 metres to the east of the tower was the first pit meant for the camp victims. Still further on, spaced at intervals of three to five metres from each another, there were three other, bigger and deeper pits (50 × 25 × 10 metres). In the beginning, camp victims were thrown into a pit without being burnt. Since the pit capacity was limited, huge excavators, so-called *bagry* (dredgers) were transported from Lvov to dig new pits all day and night.

A total of six watch towers were erected within the area of the camp, five of which were located behind the fence. Of these, four were built in the corners, and the fifth one at the Totenjuden barracks. The last tower was situated in the middle of the death centre. Their height was established after the war to be about eight metres. Some of them were equipped with searchlights, and all of them had automatic-gun stands.

The area around Treblinka was not mined, as was the case with Sobibor. The whole camp was double-fenced with barbed wire entanglements. The first line consisted of three-to-four-metre-high walls of barbed wire spread on wooden poles and thickly woven from the outside with pine twigs. A hedge was then planted along those walls, behind which there was a three-metre ditch circling the centre. Beyond this was a 40–50-metre belt of even ground, which gradually turned into forest. At the border of the area, in spring 1943, a row of anti-tank stacks called 'Spanish horses' was hidden, which were strengthened with steel rods tied with wire. Behind this area was the last outer wall of barbed wire.

Along the sandy road from Malkinia to Treblinka several information boards were erected, with notices prohibiting anyone from entering the forest. Anyone who approached the centre was to be shot immediately by the Ukrainian patrol or the guards from the towers, if the distance involved was shorter than a kilometre.

On 7 June 1942, Dr Irmfried Eberl, the kommandant of the camp, officially informed Dr Heinz Auerswald, the superintendent of the Warsaw ghetto, that Treblinka II would be ready to accept the first transport of 'resettlers' on 11 June.

The finishing touches to the building work on Treblinka were made at the end of June 1942.

PLAN OF TREBLINKA II CAMP

The general overview of the camp can only be reconstructed today on the basis of witnesses' reports because after an uprising at the camp and subsequent demolition of some buildings, a decision was made to close Treblinka II.

The first reliable data about the appearance of the camp and its regulations was passed on to local farmers by Ukrainian guards during trips to nearby villages to buy alcohol and visit women. Subsequent reports came from the fugitives who managed to escape from Treblinka after the uprising in June 1943.

The diagram reproduced in Appendix 4 seems to be the most plausible of all existing plans of the Treblinka extermination camp: all witnesses, both surviving prisoners and living members of the camp personnel, approved it. At the Düsseldorf trial of the camp kommandant, Franz Stangl, the accused, when asked his opinion of the layout, stated that it was 'absolutely correct'. Reproduced here, it is based on the work of Manfred Burba in his book *Treblinka* (Lokheide, 1995).

NOTES

1. Jeremiah 4:13.
2. The labour camp Treblinka I (*Der SS un Polizeiführer im Distrikt Warschau: Arbeitslager Treblinka*) was located near the sandpit at the edge of the forest, and it was about 1.5 kilometres from the death camp. It operated from June 1941 until 23 July 1944. About 2,000 prisoners (mainly Poles, although there were also some prisoners of Jewish origin, both from Poland and abroad) lived in wooden barracks situated in the forest. They worked at the nearby gravel pit, at unloading freight trains at the Treblinka station, at road construction, and at tree felling. From April to June 1942, a group of prisoners dug foundations at the site of Treblinka II death camp. The executions of the prisoners were carried out both in the camp itself and in the nearby forest. On 23 August 1944, due to the approach of the Soviet Army, over 500 Jewish prisoners were shot. In the first days of August, the last group of 20 Polish prisoners was murdered. A total of about 10,000 prisoners survived the camp.
3. SS-Hauptsturmführer Richard Thomalla, a civil engineer, was born in Annahof in Silesia. He supervised the construction of the death camps in Sobibor, Treblinka and Belzec on behalf of the SS. Despite the fact that his name is always connected with the above-mentioned places, Thomalla himself was present at the camps only during the construction works – witnesses agree that he left immediately upon their completion together with the staff and equipment under his command.
4. Teodor van Euppen was an aristocrat holding the title of baron. At the labour camp in Treblinka where he was the kommandant, he had a stable for his horse and a pack of hunting dogs. His favourite entertainment was trampling prisoners lying on the ground with his horse's hooves.
5. Heinz Auerswald was a lawyer by education, a member of the NSDAP from 1930, and a member of the SS from 1933. Initially a non-commissioned police officer, he served as the *Kommissar für den Judischen Wohnbezirk* in the Warsaw ghetto from May 1941. He was the author of the project of gradual starvation of the ghetto population, and of the reduction of its area, which led directly to the deterioration of the (already horrendous) sanitary conditions, and consequently to the death of thousands of its inhabitants. After the war, German prosecutors interrogated him, but he was never brought to answer for his actions.
6. The witness was employed at the station in Malkinia. On 1 June 1942, he received the order to build a branch line from the old railway siding, which lead to the gravel

pit, to the site of the newly constructed camp.

7. This testimony is contained in Z. Łukasiewicz *Obóz Zagłady Treblinka* (Warsaw: PIW, 1946), p. 8.
8. Jan Sułkowski, a bricklayer by profession, was sent to the Treblinka labour camp on 19 May 1942. He was sent there for 'evading work'. He helped on the construction of the death camp, and was released in the summer of 1942.
9. The testimony quoted according to Z. Łukaszewicz, *Obóz zagłady Treblinka*, p. 9.
10. All of the Jewish kommandos with their functions, clothing, and supervisors are described in Chapter 3.
11. SS-Unterscharführer Willy Menz, the infirmary's supervisor, and his assistant, SS-Unterscharführer August Miete. There will be more about both of them in the subsequent sections of this book.
12. Max Bielas was knifed to death by the prisoner Meir Berliner on 11 September 1942.
13. A. Donat, *Death Camp Treblinka* (New York: Holocaust Library, 1979), p. 274.
14. Z. Łukaszewicz, *Obóz Zagłady Treblinka*, p. 9.
15. The Jewish kommandos are described in detail in Chapter 3.

3 • SS-Sonderkomando Treblinka II and its Personnel

> *They seize bow and spear;*
> *They are cruel and have no mercy;*
> *Their voice roars like the sea,*
> *And they ride on horses,*
> *Arrayed as a man for the battle*
> *Against you*[1]

TREBLINKA II EXTERMINATION CAMP WITHIN THE ADMINISTRATIVE SYSTEM OF THE THIRD REICH

SS-Sonderkommando Treblinka,[2] which was the official name of the camp, was – like other centres – directly subordinate to SS-Brigadeführer Odilo Globocnik, who co-ordinated Operation Reinhard and represented the SS-Reichsführer in that territory. It was an exception, as all concentration camps were usually subject to the general inspectorate for concentration camps (Inspektion der Konzentrationslager). It was Globocnik who could decide on any changes aimed at making the work of the camps more efficient, such as the replacement of the camp kommandant, transportation system, selection of personnel, etc. He had full jurisdiction on these matters. His deputy and 'guardian' of the T4 personnel 'lent' for the purposes of Operation Reinhard on behalf of the SS was SS-Hauptsturmführer Hermann Höfle. Kommandants of all three extermination camps were subordinate to him. He was also responsible for the smooth transport of victims. Christian Wirth played a different role in the whole project. Officially, he was a technical inspector; in fact, he supervised all extermination centres in a direct way. He travelled endlessly from one camp to another checking that things were going according to his plan. His involvement did not go unnoticed by Himmler, and Wirth was granted awards and promotions.

Official documents used a code name for the camp, namely

'T II', which could be found in consignment letters for transports directed there, and a report written by SS-Brigadeführer Jürgen Stroop about the liquidation of the Warsaw ghetto.[3]

THE GERMAN PERSONNEL

The camp (Treblinka II) was divided into two parts:

- Camp no. 1, the administrative and economic section; it occupied five-sixths of the total area of the camp
- Camp no. 2, called the 'Totenlager', or the site of the killing

Both parts had their own kommandants, who were subordinate only to the kommandant of the whole camp.

The first kommandant, or rather the supervisor of the construction of Treblinka II, was the boss of the SS Construction Board and Police, Hauptsturmführer Richard Thomalla, who came there from Sobibor in April 1942. Having finished the foundations, in July he left Treblinka after handing the camp over to a medical doctor and SS-Unterscharführer, Irmfried Eberl. It was the first and only case during the history of the Third Reich of a doctor serving as kommandant of a death centre or concentration camp. Eberl, like many other people involved in Operation Reinhard, was an Austrian from Bregenz. He started his career in the Brenberg Medical Centre, near Hanover, where experiments with the euthanasia of old people were first initiated. He co-operated closely with Wirth and was one of the enthusiastic proponents of the T4 programme. The institution for the mentally ill in Brandenburg on the Havel, which he directed, continued its criminal activity until the end of 1940. It was there, in December 1939, that the first attempt was made to use carbon monoxide as a means of killing people; a method subsequently used in the gas chambers of Treblinka. The next step in Eberl's 'career' was an experimental extermination camp in Chelm, where he was a kommandant for a brief period. From Chelm he was moved to Treblinka, where the extermination camp was under construction.

As it turned out, Dr Eberl's 'experience' proved useless in the new post. Because of a lack of co-ordination between the cleaning service and the Jewish work kommandos, the camp descended into a state of chaos. As an indication of the situation in the camp in its first weeks, Yitzhak Arad, one of the foremost experts on the subject, quotes a report by a Jew, Oskar Berger, who arrived there in August 1942:

> When we were unloaded, we noticed a paralyzing view – all over the place there were hundreds of human bodies. Piles of packages, clothes, suitcases, everything in a mess. German and Ukrainian SS-men stood at the corners of the barracks and were shooting blindly into the crowd. Men, women and children, all fell down bloodstained. The air was filled with cries and despair. Those who did not get wounded were forced towards the open gate, having to jump over the killed and the wounded in order to reach the square fenced with barbed wire.[4]

The confusion was caused by the fact that the camp and its staff were not ready to accept such huge transports between July and September 1942. Because of repair work on the railway from Warsaw to Sobibor, far more trains arrived at the camp than it was prepared to 'accept'. Estimates give the number of 300,000 people (including 250,000 from Warsaw[5]) killed in the camp during that period.

As the situation in the camp reached its most critical point, towards the end of August, Wirth and Globocnik visited Treblinka. As a result of the inspection Eberl was dismissed from his duty and his position was given to Franz Paul Stangl, an Austrian policeman who had previously been the kommandant of Sobibor, and who had been promoted to the rank of SS-Hauptsturmführer[6] for his 'achievements' there.

Franz Paul Stangl was born on 26 March 1908 in a small Austrian village called Altmünster, into the family of a night-watchman. At first he worked as a tailor, then he became a policeman. In 1936 he joined the Nazi Party, which was illegal at that time. After the annexation of Austria by Germany he was transferred to the mental asylum in Hartheim near Linz, where he was supposed to supervise the euthanasia operation on behalf of the police. His participation in the T4 operation was awarded with another promotion. In 1942 he assumed command of the Sobibor extermination camp, where he showed his great organizational skills and a sense of duty and discipline. Since the situation in Treblinka was so critical, it would require all of Stangl's skills to set right.

On taking up the position of kommandant of Treblinka II, Stangl suspended transports for three days to give him time to 'tidy up' the camp. In a short time, he managed to build proper relationships with his subordinates, a feat that had never been accomplished by his predecessor. The new head was approachable and understanding towards his staff. He allowed them a lot of freedom of action, but he demanded absolute obedience in following his orders. Stangl would walk round the camp wearing a white uniform[7] and holding a leather whip. No detail was too small to escape his attention. The prisoners called him 'the white death', because SS men or Ukrainians often killed people in his presence to emphasize their devotion to 'the cause'.

His deputy, the kommandant of camp no. 1, and since August 1943, the kommandant of the whole camp, was SS-Untersturmführer Kurt Hubert Franz, born in Düsseldorf in 1914, into the family of a minor merchant. At the age of 14 he left school and started work as a cook's assistant in a local hotel. In 1932, he acquainted himself with Hitler's theories, and became an eager disciple. In 1936 he joined the German Army, but he was not a good soldier and after two years he left the Wehrmacht to serve in the SS, where he became the member of the 'skull troops', the so-called *Totenköpfverbande*. Those were special SS units trained for guarding functions in concentration camps. Franz was assigned to the Buchenwald camp for a year. In 1939, he was secretly proposed for participation in the T4 programme; a post he gladly accepted. After taking the oath, he went to the mental asylum in Grafeneck. From there he was subsequently transferred first to Hartheim and then to Sonnenstein. When he was released from T4, at the beginning of 1942, he was placed within the group allocated to Globocnik to build and administer the extermination centres in the Polish territories. In spring 1942, he was transferred to the new camp in Belzec, where he was given the post of deputy to the kommandant. Together with Globocnik and his faithful dog Bari, he came to Treblinka in August 1942, where he filled the same post as in Belzec until the uprising in 1943.

Franz's duties included efficient unloading of transports,

supervision of the Jewish work kommandos and the quick transfer of undressed and shaven prisoners to the second part of the camp. Undoubtedly, he was the most terrifying of all the German personnel of the camp. As deputy commandant, the second most important man in the camp, he tried to highlight his position and prove his worth to everybody at any cost. Witnesses agree that not a single day passed when he did not kill someone. He was tall and well dressed, and his boots were always very clean. There is no doubt that he was a sadist.

> The beautiful dog is standing by him. ... St Bernard dog.[8]
> ... The noble dog, trained in a special way by his master, becomes a wild beast acting on his orders and acting like him. It used to bite out buttocks and genitals. It tore bites of flesh from human bodies.[9]

Franz was called 'The Doll'[10] because of his appearance. Witnesses agree that he was an unusually handsome man.

Camp no. 1 included an 'infirmary', where the old, sick, incapable and crippled were exterminated. The positions of head and deputy head of this place were filled by SS-Unterscharführer Willi Mentz and SS-Unterscharführer August Miete. SS-Unterscharführer Karl Petzinger from Leipzig was the kommandant of camp no. 2, meaning the site of the killing. He was the person responsible for the extermination of all the people arriving at the Totenlager. He supervised the gas chambers at work, the dredgers for digging collective graves, and the Jewish workers who transported and burned the bodies of victims. His position was taken over by a newly arrived SS-Oberscharführer, Emil Ludwig. Gustav Münzberger and Fritz Schmidt were responsible for the proper functioning of the gas chambers. The whole Ukrainian crew came under the command of SS-Unterscharführer Willi Post.

In all, the German personnel included about 14 people. All of them were SS members recruited from the 'graduates' of the T4 programme, and they belonged to a special group appointed by the Office of the Reich to participate in Operation Reinhard. They had no frontline experience and they filled only management positions in Treblinka: supervising the construction of the centre, then the work done by the Ukrainians and Jewish kommandos, then taking care of the extermination process of Jews.

Each German, before starting work in the centre, took a solemn oath and signed a special declaration that he would keep secret everything he saw. Each one of them was held responsible by the kommandant, who had the right to punish anybody guilty of negligence with several days of detention, or in extreme cases dismiss him from the camp. The regulations were not extremely severe, and the Germans' power within the camp was quite unlimited – they were masters of life and death for both the Ukrainians and the Jewish workers.

It is worth noting that among the German personnel in Treblinka and other centres of extermination, there were no German women, although they had participated in the T4 operation as nurses.

SS men resided in specially prepared quarters. They wore the grey front uniforms of the Waffen SS, without the symbol of their native unit. They were armed only with personal handguns and leather whips. In a special barracks called 'The Arsenal', a few automatics and a box of grenades were stored in case of emergency. In addition, a small armoured vehicle was parked not far from the kommandant's building. This could be used both to send valuables to Warsaw and to strengthen the defensive capability of the centre. The official monthly remuneration was 58 marks, but for each day in the camp the employees received a bonus of 18 marks. A month's pay, together with the bonus, amounted to about 600 marks. Additionally, each member of the German personnel had the right to three weeks' leave every three months.

The German personnel, with few exceptions, such as Otto Horn,[11] did everything they could to hide their greatest weakness – namely, their small number – by wildly brutal and cruel behaviour towards the victims arriving in transports and the Jewish workers. Treblinka could put forward only 120 poorly armed men (including 15–20 SS men, who had never been at the front) against the transports of sometimes up to 2,500 Jews. Thus it may be concluded that the camp personnel, including the Ukrainians, behaved in an extremely brutal way because it was the only method of controlling a group of people 20 times larger, who within 30 minutes would become victims of the centre.

The great majority of Germans among the Treblinka personnel were young men aged 26–30, mostly married and with small children. They considered themselves special human beings, who had been given a difficult and responsible mission by the Führer. SS-men debated with Engineer Galewski, the 'camp elder' or kommandant, about the superiority of the German race and the German nation, about their sophisticated culture and the coming new order in Europe. They forced prisoners to organize choirs and orchestras, to dance, play football and box. Their commanders felt compassion for them in their hard service and they often sent them to Germany on leave. The German camp staff were concerned about their own well-being, and constantly worked on improving their living conditions. They tried to keep their barracks looking nice, by planting and tending flower gardens.

The following list includes the names of those members of the Treblinka II extermination centre:

Kommandants

Irmfried Eberl, MD
SS-Hauptsturmführer Franz Stangl
SS-Obersturmführer Kurt Franz

Camp personnel

Biala, Max
Bredow, Paul
Floss, Herbert
Hingst, August
Hirtreiter, Josef
Horn, Otto Richard
Küttner, Kurt
Lambert, Hermann
Ludwig, Emil
Matthes, Arthur
Mentz, Willy
Miller
Miette, August
Münzberger, Gustav
Petzinger, Karl
Post, Willy
Rotner
Rum, Albert

Sadie, Otto
Schmidt, Fritz
Sidow
Seidler, Kurt
Suchomel, Franz

THE UKRAINIAN GUARDS

The Ukrainian personnel of SS-Sonderkommando Treblinka numbered between 90 and 120 guards. Their commander was Ivan Rogoz, who was appointed by SS-Unterscharführer Willie Post. The majority of the Ukrainians were former Red Army soldiers who had been taken prisoner during the Russian campaign. They were offered the chance to co-operate with the SS, to which they readily agreed, probably because of the appalling living conditions in their prisoner-of-war camps. They arrived at the centre after special training in the Trawniki SS camp, which was both a labour camp and a training camp. Their task in Treblinka was to ensure both internal and external security. They were divided into squads, which were headed by Ukrainians of German origin (so-called *Volksdeutsch*).

The duties of the majority of Ukrainians consisted of supervising the efficient extermination of transports of victims and guarding the camp. Day and night, Ukrainian patrols moved indefatigably around the centre and its surrounding area, searching for those who were reckless enough to approach the camp too closely and who failed to follow the instructions posted on boards along the road. On the watch towers their fellow countrymen performed similar duties, armed with heavy machine-guns and searchlights to seek out anybody who might stumble upon the appalling secret hidden in the forest.

The duties were not identical for everyone. Based on the witness reports and Ukrainians' accounts we know about some people whose duties in Treblinka were particularly loathsome. Two operators of a gas chamber serve as an example here. Their names are given: Nikolaj Marchenko and Ivan Demianiuk, called Ivan the Terrible, who treated the people facing death with extreme cruelty. The former was short and pale, the latter tall and broad-shouldered. Nikolaj 'with eyes nice and gentle' tortured victims entering the chamber with a thick pipe; Ivan hacked those who were hesitant to enter the gas chamber with his long cavalry sabre. He cut off their hands, he chopped at their naked bodies. He tore small children from the arms of their mothers and ripped them in half.

When a transport arrived, the Ukrainians had to do their best using any means available to ensure the steady progress of the whole operation. On duty they were armed only with old German guns and leather whips. On exceptional occasions they could use Finnish machine-guns and grenades stored in the camp arsenal. Their uniforms were dark green, with black caps. From autumn 1943 those uniforms were replaced by black ones.

As the sorting kommandos recovered masses of valuables, the Ukrainians often attempted to 'trade' or steal precious items from the camp so that they could buy alcohol from the local villagers and pay prostitutes for their services. The Germans quickly cottoned on to this and the Ukrainians were forbidden, by the personal order of the kommandant, to communicate with Jews without the consent and presence of a member of the German personnel. The kommandant had the right to punish a disobedient Ukrainian guard with whipping or even death.

The following reports were given by Ukrainian guards (*wachmanns*) who, when caught after the war, told the Polish court about the centre.

Piotr Dmitrenko

> Oberwachmann[12] announced that we were *wachmanns* who were to guard Jews so that none of them could escape from the Treblinka centre. ... I worked three shifts during 24 hours; each one of us worked eight hours per day. ... When transports came, Germans selected a committee from among Jews; they brought their own *volksdeutsch* and secured the pavement to the gas chamber leaving us at its end. I stood where I was ordered. ... I stood at the pavement, and the Germans were behind us with weapons and grenades.[13]

Nikolaj Osychanski

> One or two of the *wachmanns* were postmen. Then there were two who were cooks. One was a driver at the

German headquarters of the camp. The other two were at the Diesel engine, which supplied the gas to the gas chambers, in which the Jewish nation was poisoned. The remaining *wachmanns*, about 200 of them, were divided into four platoons. I was in the second one, and our platoon served at the observation posts[14] and inside the camp. Near the fence dividing parts three and four there was a barracks, in which the Jewish people were getting undressed before going to extinction. There was a pavement leading from that barracks to the gas chambers. The pavement was up to fifty metres long and four metres wide, surrounded by a barbed wire fence up to two and a half metres high and woven with fir-tree twigs. Outside of the pavement, and around the chambers there stood armed *wachmanns* on guard from the mentioned squads, while the poisoning of Jews was going on, so that the Jews walking to extinction did not break through the fence and get out of the camp. … Each *wachmann* going on a pass was informed by the kommandant himself that if anyone reveals the secret of the Treblinka centre, he was going to die.[15]

In the conclusion of Teodozy Melnik's testimony,

Having arrived at the centre I received a gun, like others, and ten pieces of ammunition. The … uniforms were dark grey after the design of German ones … In the centre Jews were killed *en masse* by means of toxic gases in gas chambers … I did my duty in the third company and I guarded the camp from the towers, also on the ground … Only one, Wanka, was at the chambers. Germans did not let us in there where the money was.[16]

This is a list of those from among the Ukrainian guards in Treblinka whose identity has been established:

Andriejew
Demianiuk, Ivan
Dmitrenko, Piotr
Fedorenko, Fedor

Goncharow, Pyotr Nazarovich
Ivanovich, Aleksander
Kostenko
Lelenko, Pavel Vladimirovich
Malagon, Nikolay Petrovich
Marchenko, Nikolaj
Melnik, Teodozy
Mikoda
Nazarovich, Pyotr
Osychanski, Nikolaj
Petrowich, Nikolaj
Pietrykow
Pilman
Rebeka
Rudenko, Wasyl
Semonowich, Ivan
Shalajew, Nikolaj
Shevchenko
Strel'tsov, Anton Ivanovich
Vasilenko, Sergey Stepanovich
Voronkow
Yeger, Aleksandr Ivanovich

THE JEWISH WORKERS

German officers selected several people from every transport to work in the camp, depending on its current needs. It was usually young and healthy males who were chosen, and professionals in the first instance: namely, carpenters, engineers, goldsmiths, cooks, tailors, shoemakers, barbers and physicians. Sometimes, when necessary, unskilled workers were also selected to work in the camp.

Women, Polish and Ukrainian, helped in the camp with cooking and washing the dishes. There were about 50 of them. Sometimes, from a group of the Jewish women who were to be exterminated, the prettiest would be selected and forced to participate in orgies organized in the camp. After a few days or weeks such girls went to the gas chambers and new ones were selected from transports. It was usually Ukrainians who performed this task, as the Germans had strict orders not to get close to any Jewish woman. Obviously, there were exceptions to the rule.

Apart from professionals, the Germans personally selected a group of strong healthy men from each transport to do all the manual work in the camp. These people were divided into kommandos, in which a certain number of skilled workers were employed, depending on the level of difficulty of a given job.

Each Jewish kommando was given its own function and had its own symbol on sleeves and knee patches. Each group's symbols were in a different colour.

Each of the work kommandos was subject to a German officer, who was in command of a particular area of the camp. The workers were directly supervised by the Germans, and sometimes also by the Ukrainian guards, but most of the time it was the so-called *kapos*, namely, prisoners appointed by Germans, who filled the supervisory role. *Kapos* were no less cruel than the Germans or Ukrainians. They constantly tried to show their dedication to the new 'masters' by treating subordinate prisoners in a totally inhuman way; thus they were hated and despised. There were those exceptions, however, who helped the prisoners, came to their rescue and made plans of escape. *Kapo* Rakowski and Zev Kurland were among those.

The person responsible for all prisoners was 'the camp elder',[17] who was selected by the Germans. He had a clearly symbolic role in the camp; at the morning and evening roll call he produced a day report to the camp commandant or his deputy.

The list below provides names of the 'camp elders' in chronological order:

Engineer Galewski[18]
Rakowski
Engineer Galewski
(After Rakowski's death, Galewski was again chosen 'the elder' by the Germans.)

Here are the names and surnames of those *kapos* whose identity has been established:

Kurland, Zev[19]
Kuba

Bloch, Zelo[20]
Posner
Monek
Blau
Jurek
Kleinbaum
Meir
Rakowski

In the Treblinka extermination camp, the total number of Jewish prisoner-workers amounted to 1,200 and this number increased or decreased to meet the then current needs of the camp.

The following section provides details of particular camp kommandos and the functions they performed.

'The Blues' – worked at the unloading ramp; they were the first prisoners to be seen by the new transport. Their task was to carry all clothes to the square adjacent to the ramp and to clear the wagons, ramp and square, which meant getting rid of the bodies and throwing them into a special pit.

'The Reds' – helped prisoners undress at the entrance to the gas chambers and pacified them. It was particularly difficult because Jews were inquisitive about their destination. More often than not a Jew from the Reds would recognize a member of his own family, a neighbour or friend. Under threat of death, however, he was not allowed to tell them where they were going and what their fate would be.

The task of the **'Lumpenkommando'** (kommando of clothes) was to sort out the belongings of the murdered. The work was extremely hard because of the huge amount of things to sort. Witnesses recall a huge square filled with piles of shoes, scattered clothes, suitcases and backpacks. These objects formed mountains reaching ten metres in height. All around the heap there were thousands of open suitcases with broken locks and the names of their owners written in oil paint. Each object had to be put into a different suitcase. Personal belongings, shoes and linen were put separately on colourful covers spread over the square. Every single item had to be carefully checked. *Kapos* had to search every piece of clothing for jewellery, gold coins and banknotes. It was forbidden to let anything with a name leave the camp. Every single thing had to be sorted out; not only according to the type of clothing but also to its quality – the worst clothes were thrown on to bed sheets, which were tied up in big bundles and carried to open storerooms. 'There were documents, birth certificates, passports, money, family photographs. Dear letters, sometimes intimate. School completion certificates, university diplomas, craft and guild certificates, physicians' diplomas. All of them went to garbage.'[21]

After the gravediggers, the Lumpenkommando comprised the most sizeable work group of approximately 700 people.

'**The Yellows**' – called *Hofjuden* by the Germans – were a group of professional workers (carpenters, tailors, shoemakers, engineers, physicians, barbers, etc.), who ran workshops that catered for the needs of the German personnel. One of the Yellows was the famous Jankiel Wiernik, a carpenter who built most of the barracks and who prepared one of the first published reports on Treblinka;[22] and the Strawczynscy brothers, who were camp tinsmiths. These people were generally respected in the camp, and their living conditions were much better than those of the other prisoners; hence their chances of survival also looked better. Members of the camp orchestra also belonged to this group.

'**Tarnungsgruppe**'[23] – was a small kommando of 15 people responsible for the daily replacement of the twigs that provided the camouflage for the barbed wire and inside the camp. They also had to replace the wooden posts between which the wire was spread. SS Sidow headed the group. This kommando was the only one that left the camp occasionally, and to prevent any escapes it was accompanied by a group of six armed Ukrainians and SS Sidow.

'**Goldjuden**' – or 'golden' Jews – dealt with sorting out money and melting gold teeth extracted from victims into gold bars. They were considered the prison elite. Their work was not very hard, as they sat in closed, warm barracks. SS-Unterscharführer Franz Suchomel held the post of their supervisor. He was a German from the Sudeten region. He could speak Czech and he employed mostly Czech Jews, who came to Treblinka from Terezin. *Goldjuden* were responsible for taking away precious objects from the people who had just arrived at the square. Another group of them walked about the sorting square and confiscated valuables from the Lumpenkommando. The prisoners had no access to the barracks in which the *Goldjuden* worked. *Goldjuden* were far better dressed than other prisoners. 'They looked like bankers rather than prisoners, with leather gloves and suitcases into which they threw the valuables collected by the prisoners.'[24]

'**Strassenbaukommando**' – road-building kommando.

'**Holzfellerkommando**' – the kommando of woodcutters.

'**Maurerkommando**' – the kommando of bricklayers.

'**Flaschensortiererkommando**' – the kommando for collecting bottles, which were gathered and transported by trains in an unknown direction in order not to leave any traces of the camp.

'**Baukommando**' – the kommando formed in order to build new barracks and modernize the camp.

'**Zaunkommando**' – the kommando for fence maintenance. They changed posts or installed new barbed wire.

'**Scheisskommando**' – or 'szajskommando'; a special group composed of two Jews who had to monitor the time each prisoner spent in the latrine. As the camp had had problems with WCs from the very beginning of its existence, Galewski, after many requests, received permission to build two latrines. Due to the fact that, as a rule, everybody spent too much time inside the latrine, 'The Doll' came up with an idea to form a special group supervising latrines. Such was the origin of the Scheiss-kommando. Two prisoners were selected; both were dressed identically in long black rabbi gowns and caps with a pompom. They received whips and alarm watches, which hung round their necks. In that way they became a privileged group, because no other prisoners were allowed to wear watches apart from the Jewish kommandant, *kapos* and *forarbeiters*. Although the time limit for the latrine was strictly determined, the kommando deliberately prolonged it for everybody and, in consequence, the latrines became a meeting place for the prisoners.

All of the above groups worked in camp no. 1, whereas in the death camp only two kommandos were employed, namely the gravediggers whose task was to empty the gas chambers and bury (and later on burn) the bodies of victims, and the so-called 'dentists', whose task was to extract gold teeth from corpses and search them for hidden valuables. The kommando of diggers consisted of several hundred workers, and their work was considered the hardest in the camp. They had to carry the corpses and throw them into the open pits.

Any offence was heavily punished in both camps, with the death penalty imposed in a more or less sophisticated way. Most frequently the victim was killed with a gunshot in the mouth. The victims were also forced by beating to open their eyes if they tried to close them. There were also frequent cases where inmates were killed with their own work tools, usually spades.

Camp physicians definitely constitute another group worth discussing. They belonged to the 'Yellows' so they were a privileged group in the camp. They occupied a separate room called the *rewirsztuba*. A few of the Treblinka doctors' names are known, namely Dr Rybak, Dr Rajzlik, and above all Dr Chorazycki,[25] who made his mark in the camp underground movement. When sickness was diagnosed among the prisoners, the doctors did their best to help. If an infection could not be stopped, or if it was likely to come to the notice of the Germans (e.g., through the weakness or incapacity of the prisoner) the sick person was placed in the *rewirsztuba*. From that moment on, it was a dramatic fight for life. The doctors did their best to save the patient, and yet SS-Unterscharführer August Miete, the infirmary supervisor's assistant, could turn up any time with an order to give the patient up. Sometimes, at the doctors' insistence, the patients were put to sleep with a lethal injection before they could be sent out to their deaths. The camp physicians were also responsible for issuing all members of the conspiracy to escape with cyanide ampoules so they could take their own lives if they were caught by the Germans:

> But you should know that the people who had the ampoules on them, until the last moment did not believe in what was going to happen to them. They left the ampoules in their clothes on the square, and naked, driven by SS-men, they ran the death path to gas.[26]

Roll calls were an essential part of camp life, one at 5 in the morning, and one at 7 pm. They were held on a special assembly square, and during each of them all kommandos were counted, punishment was handed out (including the death penalty) for those guilty of any offence during the day, and selections were made. The bodies of those who were killed on a particular day had to be brought to the square by their kommando coworkers, so that the number of prisoners in every work group was correct. Even if one prisoner was missing, the whole group was decimated. After each roll call the song 'Goralu czy ci nie zal' ('Highlander, don't you miss it') was sung, as well as the camp hymn, entitled 'Fester Schritt'.

The hymn music was composed by a Treblinka prisoner, a

Czech Jew Walter Hirsz, and the words were in German:

> Fester Schritt und Tritt
> Und der Blick grade aus
> Immer mutig und treu
> In der Welt geschaut
>
> Darum sind wir heute in Treblinka
> Das unser Schicksal ist tara-ra
> Darum sind wir heute in Treblinka
> Und gestellt in kurzer Frist
>
> Wir hören auf den Ton des Kommandanten
> Und folgen ihm auf den Wink
> Wir gehen jeden Tritt und Schritt zusammen
> Für alles, was die Pflicht von uns verlangt
>
> Die Arbeit soll alles hier bedeuten
> Und auch Gehorchsamkeit und Pflicht
> Wir werden weiter, weiter leisten
> Bis das kleine Glück gibt einmal ein Wink
> Hu-Ha![28]

Each prisoner had to have a cap, regardless of the season or clothes. Caps were used in many ways. They were taken off when a prisoner passed by SS. The prisoners had to have them on at the roll call; they had to take them off when the Block kommandant made a report to the Germans responsible for the barracks in which the prisoners lived in. The command 'micen ap'[27] was heard several times during the roll call. Every time an SS passed by, prisoners had to stand to attention, take their cap off and say 'Ich melde gehortz am'.[29] On the German order prisoners had to hit their thigh with their cap. This action was supposed to produce a given sound. Quite often the Germans were not satisfied with the sound of smacking so prisoners were kept for hours on the square to practise smacking their thighs with caps. It was only the camp elder Galewski who had the privilege of not having to hold the cap at thigh level, but holding it against his chest with the left arm.

The Jewish workers were not obliged to follow any clothing rules. Apart from the cap and kommando badges, everybody selected something for themselves from among the hundreds of thousands of items of clothing left by the murdered victims. In autumn and winter people wore boots, warm jackets and thick caps; in spring and summer the clothes were substantially lighter. However, every 'Yellow' prisoner wanted to 'show off' his occupation, and prove with his clothes that he was important in the camp. Consequently, artists wore wide-brimmed hats; physicians of both sexes wore white uniforms so that they could be easily recognized from a distance. There were no requirements as far as hair or beard length was concerned; Jews were allowed to use the services of the camp barbers.

In the beginning, the work kommandos were frequently 'replaced' with new workers. Many transports came to Treblinka at that time, and finding both skilled and unskilled workers was not a problem. After March 1943, however, fewer and fewer transports came, so the life expectancy of the Jews working in the camp increased unexpectedly. It allowed closer contacts among them, which in consequence led to the creation of an underground organization in the camp.

NOTES

1. Jeremiah 6:23.
2. A special Treblinka unit.
3. Stroop mentions Treblinka in the entries of 25, 26 April, 13 and 24 May, 1943. They are quoted here: 'The total extermination could not be conducted [today] because of the darkness. I will try to get the train to T.II. If I fail, extermination will continue tomorrow'; 'previously mentioned transport to T.II has been successful'; 'In result of the conducted action Wehrmacht caught 327 Jews. They will be sent to T.II'; and the most shocking report:

   > Of the total of 56,065 Jews, about 7,000 were destroyed as a result of the action conducted in the former Jewish quarter. 6,929 Jews were destroyed ['vernichtet' in the original version] by shipment to T.II, so a total of 13,929 Jews were destroyed. It is estimated that apart from the number of 56,065, additionally five to six thousand Jews were destroyed by explosion and fire.

   A copy of the original Stroop Report can be found at www.holocaust-history.org, translated from German into English by Gordon McFee.
4. A. Yitzhak, *Belzec, Sobibor, Treblinka: The Operation Reinhard Death Camps* (Bloomington, 1999), p. 84.
5. Figures taken from the preface to S. Willenberg, *Bunt w Treblince*, p. 115.
6. Dr Irmfried Eberl did not take any higher position until the end of the war. In 1948, for fear of arrest, he committed suicide.
7. This uniform was mentioned by all witnesses. Stangl himself claimed that he wore it because of the heat in Sobibor.

8. Bari, or Barry according to English sources, was not a purebred Saint Bernard. On the basis of the witness report of an expert professor L., the Director of the Max Planck Institute in Seewiesen (the surname can be found in the files of the court proceedings in Düsseldorf against Kurt Franz and other members of the Treblinka personnel, dated 2 September 1965), it was established that dogs of such mixed breed have a greater sense of devotion to their master than dogs of pure blood. Because the dog was aggressive only in the company of Kurt Franz, it was concluded that Franz purposefully aroused aggression towards other people in the animal. It was also established that the parts of the human body that the witnesses stated had been bitten by the dog were normal spots for a dog of this size to attack a human. As a result of this testimony, Franz was released from the charge of training the dog to attack prisoners' genitals.

9. S. Willenberg, *Bunt w Treblince*, pp. 10–11.

10. 'Die Puppe' in German.

11. Otto Richard Horn worked at body-burning. He had been a nurse in the T4 operation. He was judged by the witnesses as the only one of the Treblinka personnel who felt compassion for them and often helped them. At the trial of the Treblinka crew in Düsseldorf, Horn was pronounced not guilty.

12. It was Ivan Rogoza.

13. Testimony given by Piotr Dmitrenko on 4 May 1953 before an investigating officer of GKBZHwP Archives, trial proceedings of the Treblinka *wachmanns*. DS. 188/67, Vol. VI, pp. 628–9, 631–7, cited by J.E. Wilczur, *Ścigałem Iwana Groźnego*, pp. 26–7, 1993 edn.

14. Watch towers.

15. Testimony given by Mikolaj Osychanski before the investigating officer of GKBZHwP Archives, trial proceedings of the Treblinka *wachmanns*. DS. 188/67, Vol. VI, pp. 671–3, 675; cited by J.E. Wilczur, *Ścigałem Iwana Groźnego*, p. 28.

16. Testimony given by Teodozy Melnik before the investigating officer of GKBZHwP Archives, on 1 May 1953, trial proceedings of the Treblinka *wachmanns*. DS. 188/67, Vol. VI, pp. 653–5; ibid., p. 28.

17. In German 'Lagerältester'.

18. His first name has unfortunately not been established. According to one version (Austrian) his name was Marceli, and he was born in Kutno on 10 October 1899. In 1928, he graduated from the electrical department of the Warsaw Polytechnic. In 1929, he married Jadwiga Litauer in Warsaw, with whom he had a daughter, Romana. Another branch of the Galewski family, however, represented by Stefan Galewski, maintains that it was his cousin Bernard who was the leader of the revolt in Treblinka. Considering the 'absolute conviction' of both sides, we will probably never learn the real first name of Galewski.

19. Zev Kurland was the supervisor at the infirmary, and one of the most tragic figures in the history of the camp. He was forced to wear a Red Cross band on his arm. He recited Kaddish every night for the Jews who had died during the day. His experiences in the camp caused him to turn grey very quickly. He joined the conspiracy right at the start, and died during the uprising.

20. Zhelomir Bloch – Czech photographer, officer of the Czech Army, member of the camp conspiracy – was transferred to camp no. 2 as a punishment. In spite of the lack of contact with the rest of the prisoners, he participated in the revolt.

21. Willenberg, *Bunt w Treblince*, pp. 13–14.

22. Jankiel Wiernik came to Treblinka in August 1942. Initially he was employed in the construction of observation towers. Then he participated in the construction of the new gas chambers and most of the significant buildings of the camp. As a result of the revolt on 2 August 1943, he managed to escape and get in touch with an organization that helped Jews – Zegota – in Warsaw. This organization enabled the members of the Jewish underground to publish, in 1944, Wiernik's shocking account of his stay in Treblinka entitled *A Year in Treblinka*. The book was published in Poland, with a print run of 2,000 copies. Microfilms of its pages were taken to

London, which made it possible to publish it widely even before the end of the war. In the years 1944–45 two editions were published in New York, in Yiddish and in English.

23. Literally 'camouflage group'.
24. Willenberg, *Bunt w Treblince*, p. 16.
25. Dr Julian Chorazycki – born in 1885 in Warsaw. He graduated from medical school in 1911. He served in the Polish Army where he was promoted to the rank of captain. He was 57 years old when he arrived in Treblinka. He was connected with the conspiracy from the very beginning. As the *rewirsztuba* was right next door to the room where the *Goldjudens* worked, Chorazycki obtained money from them for the possible purchase of weapons. Unfortunately, the *wachmann* who was to do this confessed the whole matter to Kurt Franz – the deputy kommandant. When 'The Doll' came to arrest Chorazycki, he took poison, not wanting to betray his comrades in the event of being tortured.
26. Willenberg, *Bunt w Treblince*, p. 27.
27. In German, 'Mützen ab!' – take off your caps!
28. The anthem of Treblinka was written by Artur Gold, and translates as follows:

> We look straight out at the world
> The columns are marching off to their work
> All we have left is Treblinka
> It is our destiny
>
> We heed the kommandant's voice
> Obeying his every nod and sign
> We march along together
> To do what duty demands
>
> Work, obedience and duty
> Must be the whole of our existence
> Until we, too, will catch a glimpse at last
> Of a modest bit of luck

29. In German, 'I report obediently.'

4 • *The Method of Extermination*

They have poured out their blood like
Water round about Jerusalem;
And there was no one to bury them.[1]

TRANSPORTS

Each transport of Jews to any extermination camp was carefully planned. The victims were usually transported by train, but lorries or even carts were also frequently used. Most transports came from Polish ghettos, especially from cities such as Warsaw, Czestochowa, Bialystok and Kielce. Others came from Germany and various other parts of Europe. Polish Jews were transported only in cattle wagons, while the Jews from western Europe travelled in luxury passenger coaches. Nazi propaganda provided an explanation as to why they had to be resettled. The rich Jews were told that, in connection with the colonization of the territories occupied by the Third Reich in the East, they would be transferred there to provide manpower in this area. Those people, who often lived hundreds or even thousands of kilometres from the Government General, did not realize that they were in danger. They thought it was better to leave than to remain among people who were prejudiced against them.

As for the extermination camps in Polish territory, their location and activities were clandestine. Consequently, very few people in western Europe were ready to believe that mass killing of the Jewish people was going on there. Thanks to a highly effective combination of propaganda and psychological tricks, Jews trustfully abandoned their homes and, together with their entire family and all their possessions, got on the trains heading in an unknown direction.

They bought the tickets and before boarding the train they presented them to the conductor. He checked them and directed the people to an appropriate coach. The railway personnel helped the Jews with their luggage. The trains on which Jews from western Europe travelled had dining and sleeping cars, and the conductors and waiters took good care of the passengers. When the train stopped at a railway station Jews were allowed to get off and go, say, to a buffet, or simply stretch their legs. The railway staff did their best to make this tedious and tiring journey more agreeable to the passengers. Enigmatic signs written in chalk on the sides of the train were the only reminders of their imminent death in an extermination camp. These signs were figures indicating the number of people in each car. In documents concerning the transport, every train was marked by a serial number preceded by the symbol 'Da'.

Polish Jews were transported in very different conditions. First, they were gathered in the main square of a ghetto. Next, they were counted and marched to the nearest railway station where a train stood waiting. The train consisted only of cattle wagons and two tarpaulin-covered wagons. The floor of the cars was covered with lime, which made the cars stuffy and difficult to breathe in. Depending on its size[2] one car could hold from 120 to 200 people. In every train there were between 39 and 60 cars. Each car had a small window barred with barbed wire. It was the only way for fresh air to enter the stuffy interior. The door was bolted from the outside. Having sealed all doors, German railway workers and SS officers would mark on the side of every car the figure indicating the number of people inside it. Every train had a report in which all the information about the transport was recorded. The report was drawn up at the point of departure by the stationmaster, and contained a list of all cars as well as the number of people in every car. According to Franciszek Zabecki, in every report there was a blank space for a destination of the train. In the case of trains travelling from abroad, the blank was filled with the words 'Nach ziel', which simply meant 'destination'. None of the stationmasters of the stations where the train heading to Treblinka stopped at filled in this blank. The staff at the Treblinka station learned about the arrival of every transport via a telegram. The telegram contained a detailed schedule of a given train. Each of these documents contained also the code of a train, which said where the transport was from. In the case of transports from the Government General the number of the train was preceded by the symbol 'PKr', while the code of trains going from Treblinka was 'Lp Kr'. The trains from Polish territories not in the Government General were marked as 'PJ'.

On 22 July 1942, Treblinka railway station received a telegram announcing that trains would start travelling to and fro between Warsaw and Treblinka. The message said that the trains would have 60 closed cars each and that they would transport deportees. They were to be unloaded and then directed back.[3] They were to bring the people sent to Treblinka from the Warsaw ghetto by Dr Heinz Auerwald, the German kommandant there.

Normally, a train needed two hours to cover the distance between Treblinka and Warsaw. This time it took six times longer, as the train stopped a number of times. About 200 men, women and children per car were travelling in this transport, packed in 60 cattle cars in the sweltering summer heat. On the sides of the cars there were figures written in chalk saying how many people were aboard. The numbers varied: 120, 150, 180 and even 200 people. They were deprived of water, food and fresh air, and forced to urinate inside the car. As a result of those conditions many of the Jews died *en route*, most of them old people and small children. The transport was heavily guarded. On rooftops and ladders of the cars stood or sat members of the SS transportation squad armed and ready to shoot. In the event, no one made an attempt to escape.

The first transport of Jews from the Warsaw ghetto left Malkinia for Treblinka in the early morning of 23 July 1942. Witnesses state that the approaching train could be heard from a long distance away. There were many machine-gun and pistol shots. SS guards were shooting almost all the time. Four SS officers from the camp and German railway workers stood waiting at Treblinka railway station. The German railway workers were to make sure that the cattle wagons were transferred efficiently to the camp compound. On the orders of the authorities a small switching engine was standing ready at the station. The train finally arrived at 9.30 am. It was a Thursday.

The station was filled with the moans and cries of thousands of people: 'You could hear cries, groans, screams, calls for water or a doctor. ... Although the day was hot, steam was coming out of the cars. People from the houses in the neighbourhood, especially women, brought buckets of water; they gave it to the thirsty people in the cars. ... At first, Germans did not react to that. They were amazed by it.'[4]

When the next transports came, the SS officers forbade anyone from giving water to the deportees or even to go near the train.[5]

At the station the first 20 wagons were disconnected from the train and the switching engine, escorted by the SS officers, pushed them to the camp compound. The other cars were kept under guard. After the wagons had been unloaded in the camp, they were taken back to the station and the next 20 were taken into the camp.

23 July 1942 marks the beginning of the murderous activity of the camp; 400 more days were to pass before the last drop of blood soaked into the Mazovian soil and its killing machine came to a halt.

Abraham Krzepicki describes in his memoirs the conditions inside a cattle truck during the transportation:

> The stench in the car was unbearable. The four corners served as a toilet. ... People paid 500 and 1,000 zloty for a mug of water. The railway personnel and the guards[6] took the money. ... I paid 500 and got a mug of water. Desperate for water I started drinking. Then a woman got to me shouting that her child had fainted. I was drinking and couldn't take the mug out of my mouth. With all her strength, the woman bit into my hand. ... I left some water and I saw the child drink it. ... It was only 7 o'clock in the morning, but you could already feel the sun and the heat was getting more and more intense. All men had already taken off their shirts and were lying half-naked in their shorts and drawers. Some women also took off their dresses and were in their underwear. ... A bit later, about 10 in the morning, through the window we saw a German who was in charge of our transport. We begged him to order to give us water, but he told us to wait patiently, as we would be reaching our destination, the Treblinka camp, in an hour at the latest. Yet our train waited until 4 o'clock. ... At 4 pm the train moved and soon we saw the Treblinka station.[7]

At the beginning of the camp's existence the arrival of transports was not coordinated, which brought about chaos. Considering the number of deportees brought to Treblinka there were far too few gas chambers. For that reason the trains had to wait long hours before they were unloaded. Maintenance works on the route between Warsaw and Sobibor aggravated the situation.

All trains travelling southwards had to be directed to Treblinka. In addition to the transport problems, Dr Eberl, who was responsible for the extermination, proved to be inexperienced and consequently the killing process was carried out in a very chaotic way. These problems added up to the 'difficulties' faced by SS-Sonderkommando Treblinka at the end of August of 1942.

Transports arrived every day until the end of 1942. There are very few surviving railway documents from this period but the witnesses (including Franciszek Zabecki, a worker at the Treblinka railway station quoted above) claim that the period from August (September) to December 1942 was the busiest in the history of the camp. At that time two to four trains arrived every day – each with 60 cars.[8] The trains came mainly from cities such as Warsaw, Radom, Kielce, Wloszczowa, Sedziszow, Czestochowa, Szydlowiec, Kozienice, Sandomierz, Siedlce, Lukow, Miedzyrzecze Podlaskie, Lochow, Grodno, Prostki, Sokolow Podlaski, Wegrowo, Sadowny and Kosow Lacki; there were transports from Pawiak (usually single cars),[9] and from abroad, e.g., from Germany, Belgium, the Netherlands, Czechoslovakia, Bulgaria, Yugoslavia, France, Austria and even Greece.

From time to time single transports containing Gypsies came to the camp; however, they were typically delivered in lorries, or carts, as were Jews from the vicinity of Treblinka.

THE EXTERMINATION OF JEWS IN TREBLINKA II: A RE-CREATION

The moment a transport arrived at the camp all SS, Ukrainians (except those who were on duty in the watch towers at that time), as well as all Jewish kommandos (apart from the 'Yellows') took up their positions. From then on every effort was directed at getting people to the gas chambers in the shortest time possible.

The train entered the camp through a special gate guarded by a Ukrainian. The guard opened the gate, let the train in and closed it. A small switching engine pushed 20 cars along the spur into the camp compound. The spur was very short, so the engine waited for the cars to be unloaded behind the perimeter. As soon as the train stopped, the Ukrainians opened all the doors simultaneously and, yelling wildly and beating the exhausted Jews, they pushed them out on to the ramp. The 'Blue' kommando immediately got down to clearing the cars of the corpses of those who had died on the way, as well as any objects left behind by the Jews. The bodies were thrown into a special pit that had been dug at the far end of the ramp. The cars were hastily hosed down with water. After they had been cleaned the switching engine took the empty carriages out of the camp to make room for the next round of cars.

Meanwhile, the people arriving in the next transport could see a small station that resembled many others they had passed on the way to Treblinka. They could see tradesmen's workshops, flowerbeds, a railway station building with a clock, a waiting room and ticket offices. In the vicinity there was an office of the Red Cross.[10] The majority of newcomers did not suspect anything. Nothing seemed to indicate the horror that was in store for them.

At the beginning of the camp's existence the kommandant or his deputy made a speech to the Jews assembled on the ramp. They were told that they would be soon sent to work further east, but due to their disastrous hygienic condition they would have to be disinfected first. They were ordered to leave all their luggage there on the spot and hand in all the money and valuables they had. Everybody was to get a towel and soap. They were reminded not to forget a deposit receipt. The speech usually met with applause, as many Jews believed that it was indeed a transit camp.

At about the same time, German officers selected skilled workers and strong young men from the transport. The type and number of people selected depended on the needs of the camp at any given moment. So as not to raise any suspicion among other prisoners, they were moved out of the square through a side gate.

However, some Jews noticed that the hands of the clock were not moving, the signpost indicating the direction of Siedlce pointed to the woods, and the railway line ended just behind the ramp. If anyone voiced suspicion about the situation, the Germans offered to show him round the camp. He ended up on a pile of corpses near the infirmary together with other bodies that were burnt there. The old and the sick met the same fate. In the same square, women were separated from men.

Sometimes the kommandant ordered that the prisoners be given buckets so that they could urinate or defecate. This was done in an attempt to speed up the work of the 'diggers'. The unit of diggers was responsible not only for burying the victims, but for cleaning the gas chambers as well. Getting victims to empty their bowels before death saved them some work.

Women went to a barracks on the left called the 'Beauty Salon'. They undressed there and then a group of Jewish barbers cut their hair short. Irrespective of the season of the year, men undressed outside. The Germans did not need their hair. Both men and women had to fold their clothes, tie their shoelaces, and fold their socks and stockings into a ball. The 'Red' kommando helped them with that. The 'Reds' also had to mollify the ones going to the gas chambers. It wasn't an easy task, especially as they often met a family member, friend or neighbour in a newly arrived transport.

Meanwhile, once the cars had been cleaned, an SS officer signalled to the engine-driver who withdrew the 20 cars from the camp, only to return 15 minutes later with another 20 packed with new victims.

The final stage of life's drama was about to start for the naked Jews. It took place on a path that was 100–120 metres long and 2 metres wide and covered with white gravel. The path was fenced on both sides. The high fences were made of barbed wire that was camouflaged with a great number of pine-tree twigs.

Jews were shouted at and called names. They ran naked, with their hands up, deprived of human dignity, to meet their tragic fate. To speed them up the SS men beat them with whips and rifle butts, and cut them with bayonets. Their bodies were torn by fierce dogs. This horrible procession was led by the so-called *Bademeister*,[11] who continually hurried them: 'Faster, faster, my children, the water's ready.'

At the end of the path stood a building with columns, modelled on an ancient classical temple. Five concrete steps decorated with basketfuls of flowers led to the entrance. Above the door there was a portal with the Star of David and the Hebrew inscription: 'Through this gate only the righteous pass.' The door itself was covered with a dark, heavy curtain, probably stolen from a synagogue. At the entrance two Ukrainian executors greeted the Jews. They operated the gas chambers. One of them was Ivan, known as Ivan the Terrible; the other was Nikolaj. They seemed to compete with each other to inflict the crueller atrocities. With his long bayonet or a cavalry sword, Ivan cut off women's breasts. His companions followed suit. Joseph Hirtreiter, an SS, specialized in murdering small children. He held them by their feet and smashed their heads on the stairs. He also enjoyed crushing babies thrown down on the floor with his boots. The Ukrainians often molested young Jewish girls before sending them to the gas chambers. They often pushed their hands or shoes in their crotch, or brutally raped them. For many of these girls it was the first and the only sexual contact in their lives.

Beaten all the time, the victims ran dutifully into the chambers through a narrow door. Inside they could free their bodies from blows at least for a while. There was a reason why the door was so narrow. That was to prevent the victims from escaping quickly in the case of a revolt. Most of the chambers were packed as tightly as possible. When there were no more standing places for adults, children were thrown on to their heads.

After the iron door had been hermetically sealed, the German kommandant called to the chamber operator: 'Ivan, give them water!' Special pumps started sucking out the air. The naked people, standing side by side on cold, orange tiles looked up, where they could see glossy shower heads. The hum of the pumps soon died down. Some people fainted because of the crush and lack of fresh air. A moment later they heard the throb of an engine starting up. From the pipes over their heads, dark, asphyxiating smoke began to appear. People screamed with horror and jerked in agony; someone often tried to break the door down, and children cried their hearts out. Carbon monoxide gradually filled the small room, relentlessly assimilating oxygen particles. A horrid invisible force pressed the victims' lungs, blocking their throats. Seconds passed but they seemed to be hours. Almost 2,000 human beings struggled desperately for their lives before giving in to the silent, noxious gas.

At the same time a special Jewish kommando was sorting the victims' goods. Their clothes, glasses, books, diaries, letters, money, often the most precious possessions they had accumulated throughout life were carefully sorted and prepared to be sent to the Third Reich. The wild screams of the slowly suffocating victims were audible not only to the persecutors, who nodded with a smile as they heard them, but also to those who were standing naked in front of the gas chambers waiting for their turn.

The Jews' desperate struggle with death continued for about 30 to 40 minutes. The voices gradually faded away to stop altogether. One of the SS came up to the door and listened. Absolute silence inside was a signal for a kommando of diggers to open the back door, through which corpses were removed. If, however, moans were still heard, the gas was not switched off.

Having made sure that everybody was dead, diggers opened the special door located in the back wall of every chamber. Next, they waited for a few minutes for the chambers to ventilate, and then got down to removing the corpses. This was a horrible task. It often happened that close people (family members, friends, etc.) held hands while they were being gassed, and as a result of rigor mortis the limbs became hard as stones. Consequently, the bodies of murdered people often had to be torn apart. Besides, most bodies were covered with urine, menstrual blood, vomit and every other possible bodily discharge.

Diggers took the corpses out to a special concrete spot adjacent to the building housing the gas chambers. Then a kommando of 'dentists' inspected the bodies to see if the dead had gold teeth or dentures. If that proved to be the case they extracted gold elements by means of cambrels, chisels or hammers. Gold elements extracted from the victims' mouths were put into jars containing acid. Germans suspected that Jews would want to smuggle their valuables to gas chambers. For that reason they ordered the dental kommando to check other body cavities using the same devices.

After they had been checked, the bodies, now even more mutilated, were returned to diggers. They dragged the victims a few metres and threw them into the pit. When the pit was full, they poured petrol in and then burned the bodies.

At the beginning there were rails leading to the pits, and wagons ran along them. The diggers put the bodies into the wagons and then pushed them towards the pit. However, due to the large number of transports, this method proved to be too slow and Germans gave it up in favour of the ones described above.

In this way, in 90 minutes, around 2,000[12] were robbed and then brutally murdered. The time necessary for this procedure (admitting, undressing, and killing such a number of people) was carefully calculated and co-ordinated with the schedules of trains coming to Treblinka.

At the beginning of the camp's operation, the corpses were disposed of in large pits dug out by huge excavators, the so-called 'dredgers', which worked night and day. From the spring of 1943, the bodies were burnt on gigantic 'grates' made up of rails. That was done following Himmler's orders. To improve body disposal process, an 'expert' in the burning of corpses came to Treblinka from Auschwitz. He was SS-Oberscharführer Herbert Floss; known to prisoners as 'Tadellos'[13] because of his constant use of this word.

THEFT OF THE VICTIMS' PROPERTY

While naked Jews were walking to the gas chambers, their fellows from the Lumpenkommando worked hard separating clothes, money and personal belongings.

All valuables and money found in clothes were taken by the 'Gold' kommando. Their work started on the ramp, where they collected the 'deposited' valuables from the people who arrived in transports. Then they went to a sorting square, where every sorting unit of the Lumpenkommando was obliged to hand over all valuables found in clothes.

Money was also sorted: 'Money that we were sorting was put in separate piles. We put banknotes, coins, dollars, pounds, gold roubles and "rubbish" (as we usually called the Polish currency) separately.'[14]

Among the prisoners who sorted things, a few specialist units were organized. Each group dealt with one kind of things. There was a group that collected bottles (Flaschensortiererkommando), others had to collect only fountain-pens, etc.

Having been cleaned in hydrochloric acid, gold teeth and dentures were handed over to a special unit of 'jewellers', whose duty was to melt them into bars.

The stolen possessions were loaded on to freight cars. Different kinds of clothes were loaded separately. Small objects such as pens, pencils, thread, etc., were put into suitcases. Franciszek Zabecki gives an account of the transporting of this unusual freight:

> … women's hair was sent, too. The load was referred to as military consignment 'Gut der Waffen SS'.[15] Everything was sent to Germany or sometimes to SS-Arbeitslager in Lublin;[16] either one car at a time or the whole train. Fifty cars were dispatched with one consignment letter on 13 September 1942 as 'Bekleidungsstücke der Waffen SS' (clothing), military transfer No. 6710002 to Lublin.[17]

The cars departed Treblinka station after SS officers had delivered military consignment letters with the address, a seal and a signature. Usually it was the same SS who did this. The consignment letters were registered in a dispatch book. They had a seal of the station, a serial number of shipment and a signature of the stationmaster:

> The cars of the train were labelled.[18] The officers checked
> if the windows were closed and the doors of the cars
> sealed. The cars waited at the station for the whole night,
> and if the transport was a big one, that continued even
> for the subsequent nights.[19]

Such a situation occurred when Jews did not manage to load all cars during a single day.

Samuel Willenberg describes the loading of stolen possessions: 'Late in the evening 20 empty cars were placed on the spur. ... Everybody took a 60-kilogram package and ran to the car as quickly as possible. Then he returned even faster and took another bundle, and so on.'[20]

The transportation of the stolen valuables proceeded in a completely different way; the station was given permission to use a special switching engine from Malkinia for this purpose. When it was needed, the German railway employees ordered the engine and it was sent down immediately from Malkinia. SS leaving the place for a few days had a car at their disposal. Nevertheless, they would order Klinzmann or Emmerich[21] to send the engine. One of the drivers was given a valuable parcel to transport in his engine to Malkinia; in Malkinia the parcel was transferred to a passenger train heading for Germany. The system of having an engine on standby was a costly one but, after all, the looted goods provided a large income for the Reich. In addition, an escorted armoured car frequently left the camp for Warsaw, and it probably carried valuables. From time to time empty freight cars were brought to the camp. They left Treblinka loaded with suitcases, escorted by a few heavily armed Ukrainians and commanded by SS officers. The cars loaded with valuables and money were sent to Malkinia (without being registered) and forwarded by train to the Reich.[22]

Another thing that should be mentioned in connection with the theft of prisoners' goods is the barter that took place between the prisoners who worked in sorting units and the Ukrainian guards. Germans stole openly but Ukrainians had to ask the prisoners for everything. As the *Goldjuden* were strictly controlled, the Ukrainian *wachmanns* exchanged goods with the prisoners from the Lumpenkommando. There were far more of them and they were not so strictly supervised; hence they had the chance of keeping some money and valuables for themselves. This is how they traded: a Jew went up to a Ukrainian guard on duty and offered him dollars, gold roubles, precious stones or other valuable objects. In exchange he asked the Ukrainian to provide products that were unavailable in the camp, e.g., bread, sausage, chocolate, a bottle of wine or vodka. Ukrainians always agreed, but they warned that in the event of any problems arising they would wash their hands of the transaction. In this way they made a deal and, usually, on one of the following evenings, in a secluded spot (behind the bushes or by the window of a barracks) the Ukrainian and the Jew met to exchange goods.

These activities cost many lives. Still, they had a lot of advantages. They allowed for an uncontrolled transfer of food to the camp (and, at the end of the camp's existence, even some weapons) for the Jewish underground organization in the camp.[23] Local people willingly did business with the Ukrainians, as it provided a constant flow of money for them. The Germans were well aware of what was going on. They even knew the families engaged in these activities.

At the beginning of the camp's existence, gangs of drunken Ukrainian guards systematically 'invaded' the villages in the neighbourhood. Soon after Stangl became the kommandant of the camp, he forbade them to carry guns when they left the camp. From then on, the Ukrainians behaved better. They were afraid that local people and members of the Polish underground would take revenge on them. However, the Ukrainians made attempts to buy weapons in local villages. One of them got drunk in a village and was arrested after returning to the camp. After searching him, the SS found a gun. He explained that he had bought a gun from a Pole in the village of Grady. After a short investigation Stangl found out that the gun had been bought from a landlord named Sansel and he arrested the whole Sansel family (about 22 men and women). They were all sent to the gas chambers.

At that point discipline and control in the camp became stricter and now the Ukrainians were subject to it as well. They were convinced that 'those who had been working in the camp since it was set up would be liquidated by the SS-men'.[24] Cases of escapes among the Ukrainians started to multiply.

NOTES

1. Psalms 79:3.
2. The witnesses mention two types of cars used to transport Polish Jews: French (they were bigger and more spacious) and Polish (smaller and less durable). A French car could accommodate up to 200 people, while in ordinary Polish ones there was room for 'only' 120.
3. F. Zabecki, *Wspomnienia stare i nowe*, pp. 38–9.
4. Ibid., pp. 38–41.
5. After the local people found out that the Jews had money, they started regular trade with them. They gave Jews water and food in exchange for money and valuables. Obviously, Germans were interested in the Jews' money and, fearing that it would be wasted, they threatened to kill those who came near the trains. However, there were still some who were not scared away and continued to trade with Jews.
6. Ukrainian *wachmanns*.
7. A. Krzepicki, '18 dni w Treblince', *Biul. ZIH*, 1962, 43/44, pp. 88–9.
8. Zabecki claims there were even five transports a day, *Wspomnienia stare i nowe*, p. 42.
9. These towns are enumerated by Zabecki, ibid., p. 42.
10. The so-called 'lazaret'.
11. Literally 'master of the bath'.
12. The differing estimates for the death toll in the gas chambers depends on whether one is referring to the original gas chambers (see above, p. 33) or to the newer building (for construction details, see below, p. 70). Page 29 describes the old building which housed three chambers, built during spring 1943. Ten new gas chambers were then built, housed in one building, although they were not used all at once. The chambers were constructed using a corridor system, that is, there was a central corridor from which the ten chambers opened up. This is the building used for gassing the victims on pp. 62 and 63. There is an added complication: in Polish the phrase, 'gas chamber', can refer to both the whole building or to individual chambers within the building.
13. German for 'great', 'perfect'.
14. Krzepicki, '18 dni w Treblince', p. 103.
15. German for 'goods belonging to the Waffen SS'.
16. The concentration camp at Majdanek.
17. Zabecki, *Wspomnienia stare i nowe*, p. 72.
18. The labels indicated the direction in which they were going.
19. Zabecki, *Wspomnienia dawne i nowe*, p. 73.
20. Willenberg, *Bunt w Treblince*, p. 36.
21. The names of German railway employees (already referred to) supervising the work of Polish stationmasters at the station in Treblinka.
22. Zabecki, *Wspomnienia stare i nowe*, pp. 74–5.
23. Almost all Jews bartered with Ukrainians.
24. Zabecki, *Wspomnienia stare i nowe*, pp. 84–5.

5 • The History of the Camp

Would He not let my few days alone?
Withdraw from me that I may have a little cheer.
Before I go – and I shall not return – to the land of
Darkness and deep shadow;
The land of utter gloom as darkness itself.[1]

TREBLINKA II FROM SEPTEMBER 1942 TO 1943

In the second half of August 1942 visitors to the camp included SS-Obersturmführer Kurt Gerstein, the head of the 'health department' (Abteilung Gesundheitswesen) of SS General Headquarters (SS-Führungshauptamt)[2] and SS-Obersturmbannführer Professor Wilhelm Pfannenstiel, the Head of the Institute for Hygiene at Marburg University. Gerstein had been ordered to check the possibility of substituting carbon monoxide with Zyklon B in the Operation Reinhard camps. Gerstein received 100 kilograms of Zyklon B[3] to demonstrate to Globocnik that it was a much better means of killing. However, Gerstein was unable to persuade Wirth to give up the method that he himself had invented. Faced with such a reaction, Gerstein returned to Berlin.

The situation in Treblinka changed radically when SS-Hauptsturmführer Franz Stangl replaced Dr Irmfried Eberl as kommandant. Franz Stangl inherited a number of problems from his predecessor. First of all, there were piles of decomposing bodies that had not been buried and heaps of clothes on the ramp. Between 25 August, and 2 or 3 September 1942, the transports were suspended. During that time additional kommandos of workmen were organized. Some 50 prisoners from the Treblinka I labour camp, together with a cohort of Jews, made up a new kommando that cleaned up the area in a very short time. Abraham Krzepicki,[4] who was one of the workers ordered to remove the bodies, recalls:

Lots of bodies that I had seen a few days earlier were still lying on the ramp. ... They were half-rotten and worms were feeding on them. ... Many bodies were falling apart, and when we were removing them from a pile the limbs would come off. That happened most often with children's bodies, as they were more delicate. ... Others picked up the heads, guts, hands and feet, which came off the bodies. Not everybody was strong enough to carry the enormously swollen bodies of those who suffocated during the transport.[5]

After the bodies had been removed and the camp tidied up, some of the workers were no longer necessary. Fifty of them joined a group of prisoners from the labour camp, and the remaining 100 were sent to the gas chamber. The ones whose lives were spared were divided into kommandos, as described in Chapter 3. It is worth noting that the *Goldjuden* kommando consisted initially of six watchmakers.

At that time the camp orchestra was organized. It consisted of seven musicians who played modern 'hits' with a mandolin and violin accompaniment. On the night of 31 August, a special concert was organized to 'celebrate the third anniversary of the outbreak of World War Two'. There were Ukrainian dances and Jewish music.

From 1 September on, there was a ban on passenger trains stopping at Treblinka station. The station received a telegram no. 234 of 27 August 1942, from Cracow confirming this. The intention behind this order may have been to ensure that train traffic did not interfere with the activities carried out in the camp. Besides, there was always the danger that somebody on a train would see something that indicated that mass killing was being carried out. The regulation could also have been intended to make escape difficult for the runaway Jews who managed to flee from trains at night, or to prevent intruders approaching the area. This order was obeyed in so far as the trains did not stop at the station, but either near the signal or somewhere on the track between the stations.

Preparations for the arrival of new transports started. From different kommandos Germans selected a group of 40 Jews who knew German. Their task was to explain to the newcomers what they should do and to pacify them. The following day another selection was carried out, and as a result 35 people stayed in this group. Five of them were rejected because they did not have 'a very optimistic tone of voice'. They were sent back to work in their kommandos.

The next transport arrived at 8 am on 8 September. Franz Stangl, the camp kommandant, personally welcomed the victims. Christian Wirth, who was staying at the camp at the time, was also present. Five hundred men were selected from the transport; their women and children were taken straight to the gas chambers. The order was given to feed the men. A group of workers who had been in the camp for a while were gathered in the square and then shot dead within half an hour.

From then until the end of December 1942, two or even three transports arrived at the camp daily. It was the busiest period in the history of Treblinka II.

Due to the large number of transports, a decision was taken to build another ten gas chambers. The construction work started at the beginning of September under the supervision of two engineers from Germany, Erwin Lambert and Lorenz Hackenholt.[6] The new gas chambers were housed in a brick building, modelled on a Greek temple. It had columns and was decorated with flower-filled vases. Above the entrance was the Star of David and an inscription in Hebrew, which read: 'Through this gate only the righteous pass.' Five concrete steps led to the massive white-painted door, which was covered with a heavy black curtain. Behind the door was a long corridor with five doors on each side. They led directly to gas chambers. Each chamber was seven by seven metres in size and 2.3 metres high. The floor was covered with tiles; walls were painted to make them easier to clean. Each chamber had two doors. The entrance door was made of steel with rubber round the edges, and closed hermetically. The other door was situated in the back wall. It looked like a huge rectangular steel window located just above the floor. Through this door the bodies of victims were removed. The floor of the chamber sloped towards this door, to make it easier to remove the bodies.

The new building was much bigger than the previous one, but the height of the chambers was lowered by 60 centimetres in comparison with the old ones. This was done to prevent children surviving the gassing, as they did on occasion in the higher-ceilinged chambers.[7] The total size of all chambers was 320 square metres, compared with just 48 metres previously. Jankiel Wiernik, a carpenter who worked in the camp, describes the construction work:

I was one of the builders. It turned out that it housed ten
new gas chambers ... After the work had been completed,
the Hauptsturmführer said to his subordinates: 'Endlich
die Judens tadt fertig.'[8] The construction work took five
weeks ... We worked from dawn till dusk under the pres-
sure of whips and rifle butts. One of the Ukrainian guards
– Woronkow – tortured us ... Every day he killed some
workers ... Every day transports arrived. The people were
told to undress immediately, and then they were marched
to the three original death chambers to meet their death.
On the way there they passed the construction site. Many
of us saw their children, wife, and family among those
victims. If anybody governed by the feeling of the utmost
pain at the sight of their beloved going to gas chambers
ran up to them, he was killed instantly.[9]

The Jews arriving from Warsaw at the beginning of September
told their fellow prisoners about 'the pot of death' that had been set
up there in an area of four square kilometres.[10]

On 11 September, a prisoner selection was carried out. New
workers were selected from the new transport; the old group of
workers was to be done away with. The selection was carried out
by SS-Scharführer Max Bielas, accompanied by yet another SS
(whose surname is not known) and a few Ukrainian guards. All
workers stood in a line expecting the worst. Bielas walked among
them choosing the shorter and weaker ones, who were to be killed.
Suddenly, one of the prisoners (his surname was Berliner) drew a
knife, left the line, ran up to Bielas and pushed the blade in his back
up to the hilt. The fatally wounded SS groaned and sank into the
arms of hastily approaching Germans and Ukrainians. What
followed was indescribable chaos:

SS-men came ... They looked petrified ... Berliner did not
even try to escape. He stood quite composed, with a
strange, mild smile in his face ... But a few minutes later
he was lying on the ground with his face smashed. Blood
flowed from his mouth[11] ... Bielas died of wounds a few
days later[12] ... Two other Jews were killed with spades.
The Ukrainians started beating people around frantically
... The kommandant ordered 'Lalka' to shoot ten Jews.[13]

Kommandant Stangl, together with Franz, beat Galewski and his deputy in front of the prisoners. That evening none of the kommandos got an evening meal. Water and meals were not given out for three days.

On the next day, 12 September, there was another selection. This time it was made by Kurt Franz himself, already known in the camp as 'Lalka'. He selected 60 people, who were shot within 20 minutes.

Transports from the Warsaw ghetto[14] came to Treblinka till 3 October. Very few men from these transports were selected to join the working units. One of the witnesses, Samuel Rajzman, arrived on 21 September. From the whole transport only two men were selected (he and another man, who was shot within the next 48 hours).

In mid-October a train arrived from Siedlce packed entirely with corpses – 60 cars filled with bodies. It turned out that the train had been stopped on the way by SS who knew where the transport was going. They murdered all the people and stole their valuables. Then they packed old clothes into the two carriages where the valuables were being transported. This was the first time in the history of the camp that somebody else relieved the butchers of Treblinka of the task of murdering and robbing the Jewish people.

On the day after the arrival of that transport, four prisoners fled from the camp under cover of morning fog. In an act of reprisal Germans shot 20 sick people in the infirmary, whom the camp doctors had, however, anaesthetized. One of those who fled was a man who Samuel Rajzman[15] had met previously. There would not be anything strange about this if it had not been for the circumstances in which they met:

> I knew a man who married a girl from Wegrow ... One day he disappeared in mysterious circumstances and was not seen by anybody. A few weeks later, however, he appeared again. He came to our shop ... He said that he had been to Treblinka and that with his eyes he saw that it was not a labour camp. They took people to gas chambers straight from the cars, and then they burnt them. A few people worked there, he was also selected to work with some other men ... Everybody thought that he had probably gone mad ... When they took me to Treblinka, a

few weeks later that guy came there again … He told me then: 'Rajzman, I'm going to try my luck in escaping again' … I asked him to visit my daughter and give her my love and the pen, which would prove that he had met me. He took the pen and disappeared … Six weeks later he came with another transport … I came up to him and he said: 'Yes, I met your daughter … I gave her your pen and you can't imagine how happy they were hearing that you were alive' … After the war I found out that he had indeed been there and met my daughter.[16]

One night in November 1942, a transport from Grodno arrived in Treblinka. The transports usually came in the daytime, but this one was different. Having realized where they were and what was in store for them, the Jews from the transport reacted violently. Two thousand men, women and children fought against a small group of armed guards of the camp. They were punished for their action – everybody was killed. Three SS were taken to a nearby hospital.

In the second half of December 1942, when the number of transports had decreased to about one a week, some people from the Treblinka I camp were transferred to Treblinka II. Food depots were empty so the prisoners did not get any food. As Christmas was approaching, a number of the SS were granted leave to go home; consequently, there were fewer personnel in the camp.

Due to the planned murder of 'useless' workers (which was Engineer Godlewski's idea), some prisoners who worked with the Flaschensortierenkommando were transferred to another kommando, which specialized in making and glazing pots.

The winter of 1942/43 was marked by famine. It was freezing cold. The sanitary conditions were disastrous. The barracks were built of wood, and in most cases there was no floor, so the prisoners were not protected from cold. The SS ordered them to warm their barracks with straw.

About mid-July 1943 transports from the Warsaw ghetto started arriving again. Because of this all the 'diggers' who had been temporarily transferred to the Lumpenkommando to sort clothes, returned to Treblinka II. From then on, from every new transport 20 men were selected to work, while 20 others who had been working up to that moment were killed to make room for the new ones.

At the end of January an epidemic of typhoid fever broke out in the camp. To prevent the spread of the disease the Germans killed anybody who seemed weakened. SS-Unterscharführer August Mitte, assisted by the 'Red' kommando, accompanied the sick to the infirmary. There, he or one of the Ukrainians killed the sick man by shooting him in the neck and threw him down into the pit. In this way, in a very short time, 300 prisoners were murdered. The majority of them had earlier been given a sleeping tablet or poisoned by the camp doctors.

Trying to protect the rest of the prisoners from executions, Engineer Galewski suggested hiding some of them in the 'stables',[17] now a clothes storehouse, in between fur coats. The Germans stayed away from this place, as they were afraid of lice. Besides, thanks to barter with Ukrainians, the Jews obtained some oranges and lemons, which helped them to stay healthy. In this way a lot of people were saved. Unfortunately, some of them, despite great care, did not recover. Nothing could be done. Day by day, hundreds of sick prisoners were removed from the barracks and the sick rooms by the 'Reds'. First, the camp doctors injected a sleeping drug. The 'Reds' carried the anaesthetized patients as far as the infirmary. However, they did not take them through the main door but laid them near the pile of burning bodies:

> A *wachmann* ... came down on the sand, loaded his machine-gun slowly, warmed his hands over the burning corpses. Then he commanded the prisoner to be put on the ground, tossed his gun and suddenly its barrel was a few centimetres away from the victim's head. And a muffled sound of a shot followed.[18]

From time to time dozens of men were selected from transports and sent to work in the Treblinka I labour camp. In exchange for them, those who were no longer able to work at mining for gravel were delivered to Treblinka II. As nobody except for staff members was allowed to enter the extermination camp, the rejected prisoners from Treblinka I, escorted by SS and Ukrainian guards, came up to the main entrance to Treblinka II and were taken from there. Next, they were counted, divided into groups of five and marched to the ramp where they were told to take off their clothes. Then they were led along 'The Way to Heaven'.

Having dealt with the epidemics, on orders of Kommandant Franz Stangl, a group of workers supervised by Jankiel Wiernik, a camp carpenter, started constructing new buildings – a laundry, a laboratory and a room for women. The building material came from some old barracks that were pulled down as they had been empty for some time as a result of the epidemics.

At about the end of February 1943, shortly after the epidemics ended, the camp was equipped with a new excavator. In order to bring it to the camp a part of the fence had to be removed. Prisoners expected that the transports would henceforth be bigger: they guaranteed a supply of food, clothing and money; but, most importantly, they meant the lengthening of the camp's existence, which raised hopes that the death sentence pronounced on them the moment they had arrived in Treblinka, would not be passed very soon. However, something different was in store.

MARCH TO AUGUST 1943

In mid-March 1943, SS-Reichsführer Heinrich Himmler visited the camp. A few members of his headquarters' staff accompanied him. All prisoners were gathered in the assembly square. With caps doffed, they stood to attention and listened to a speech by Eichmann,[19] who said that they had been selected to work and they would be fine. Eichmann said that Germans would organize a new Jewish country and all the valuables taken away from Jews would be used for Jewish purposes. All the prisoners would be taken into the German Army to form a disciplinary unit (Ordnungsdienst).

The next person to address the prisoners was Franz Stangl, SS-Hauptsturmführer and camp kommandant. He said that there were new regulations in the camp. Henceforth, if somebody were caught with gold or money, he would be killed. If a prisoner had food that was not from the camp, he would be shot dead. The same sentence would be passed for damaging things formerly belonging to the murdered. Fifty lashes would be the punishment for incorrectly carrying out an order given by Kommandant Godlewski or a prisoner foreman. For an offence against a *forarbeiter* they would get 50 lashes; for an offence against a barracks leader 25 lashes. Also, from that day on, there was to be a complete list of prisoners, and everyone would have their own file in which all offences would be recorded.

After the assembly all prisoners went to their barracks, where barracks' leaders were waiting for them. They took down prisoners' names and surnames. All registered prisoners were given an eight-centimetre triangular leather badge with coloured material sewn on to them. The badges were numbered. Prisoners were divided into groups according to where they lived. The first barracks got blue and green triangles; the second got the red ones.

On Himmler's order, the name of the camp was changed to 'Obermajdan Treblinka'. On the same day, Germans started shaving prisoners' hair. This was to be done every 20 days. The recent epidemic was probably the reason for this decision. As new transports were not expected and Germans wanted to keep the camp open they realized that sanitary conditions had to be improved. The decision to keep the camp working was connected with the plans to liquidate the Warsaw ghetto. The Treblinka II extermination camp was to play a major part in this.

Another result of Himmler's visit was the renovation of the ramp. Its appearance was to be altered to imitate a railway station. There had been plans to do this much earlier, just after the camp was set up. But the idea was given up in favour of improving the methods of extermination. Directions were painted on white boards: 'Nach Bialystok und Wolkowisk';[20] and a three-metre board with the new name of the camp appeared. A model of a clock was made of wood and was placed high on the front wall of 'the station', which in reality was a storehouse where victims' belongings were kept. On the walls of this building were signs which read: 'First Class', 'Second Class', 'Third Class', 'Waiting-room' and 'Ticket-office'.

The question of the mass graves of Polish officers shot in the spring of 1940 in the wood in Katyn was the hottest topic of conversation in the camp at that time. The officers had been shot by the NKVD (Russian secret police). The subject was discussed by SS, Ukrainians and prisoners, even during Himmler's visit. It probably was because of this 'discovery' and its consequences that Himmler ordered the burning of camp victims' bodies (both of those who were shot and those who were gassed). This meant that all prisoners who arrived in Treblinka would have to be burnt after being gassed. Moreover, all mass graves from the first period of the camp's existence were to be destroyed to obliterate all traces. Thus, the rotting bodies had to be exhumed and burnt.

It soon became apparent that this change of policy was the reason why the huge excavator had been brought to the camp. A few days after Himmler's visit, a tank of oil was delivered to Treblinka II. The next day, an experiment was carried out in burning corpses. The first attempt was unsuccessful. Jankiel Wiernik, who worked at Treblinka II, described it thus:

> It turned out that women burnt more easily than men did. So they were burnt first as kindling ... Every day the number of burnt bodies was registered ... Male corpses did not burn. So the workers poured some petrol on the bodies and thus burnt them. When a plane was spotted in the sky, the work was stopped and the bodies were covered with fir tree so that nobody in the plane would notice ... When a pregnant woman was burnt, a belly would burst and the child would get outside and burn in its mum's lap.[21]

The process of burning corpses was a failure; it dragged on endlessly. Expert advice was called for; SS-Oberscharführer Herbert Floss came to Treblinka from Auschwitz. A few days after his arrival, rails were delivered on flat cars. In Treblinka II prisoners started laying concrete foundations and a grid was made up of five or six rails each 25–30 metres long arranged in such a way that they made a grate. Under this structure a fire was started. First, Jews working as 'diggers' arranged corpses on the grate. However, when it became evident that the system was not efficient, excavators were used to get the corpses out of mass graves and deposit them on the above-mentioned grates. A grate could accommodate 3,000 bodies.

A few days later, from behind a sandy embankment which separated the living camp from the death camp, the prisoners saw the upper part of an excavator. It was being used to build an embankment some five metres high.

> From its open jaws bodies fell down ... Then the flames burst and the smoke was dozens of metres high ... The machine dug out the bodies from the graves and threw them down on the grates. The stench of burning and decomposing bodies was in the air all around the place ...

> Often from the teeth of the machine hung guts that had got stuck there.[22]

After the bodies had been burnt, 'diggers', now more numerous (as they had been reinforced with prisoners selected from Treblinka I), swept away all that remained on the grates. This was usually ash with some fragments of bones that had not burnt. It was all crushed with hammers, then mixed with soil and thrown into the graves. 'Diggers' sometimes disobeyed and put bones and fragments of bodies into the graves, covering them with a layer of sand.

Now the process of burning progressed smoothly and the camp was ready to receive new transports.

At the end of March 1943 transports from Bulgaria arrived. People on these transports were rich and they brought a lot of bread, smoked lamb, cheese, etc.

> The camp used things brought by victims, and consequently we got better meals … They were murdered in a very cruel way. All through the night small amounts of gas were pumped into the chambers. They suffered for a long time before they breathed their last.[23]

Because of the new transports, the prisoners had hope again. They knew they were indispensable for performing certain tasks and their brothers' death spared them death from hunger, too. When transports did not come, they were given just one meal a day.

Following the transports from Bulgaria, a train arrived from Greece. The newcomers onboard had labels on their luggage reading 'Saloniki'. Among them there were many intellectuals, professors and assistant professors – wealthy people. Greeks were transported in freight cars, but there were only a few dozen people in each. The cars were not locked or sealed. All the Greek Jews were well dressed and had masses of luggage: eastern carpets, rugs, huge amounts of food, lots of spare clothing, equipment, gadgets. None of the Greeks had any idea where they were or what would become of them.

The situation in the camp changed radically. The camp storehouses were full again. They were stuffed with dried lamb, olive oil, tinned meat, sardines, wines, cigarettes and other rare items.

The Germans shared in the happiness of the prisoners, saying to them that 'the hard times had ended for the camp, and that we would never be hungry and that there would be many such transports in the future'.[24]

The SS knew that more transports from Greece were expected to arrive in Treblinka soon. Shortly after the transport from Saloniki described above, several others were sent to Treblinka. Thanks to these transports the prisoners did not feel hungry for some time; they even got three cigarettes a day.

Transports from the Warsaw ghetto were still arriving. With one of them arrived Artur Gold, a well-known musician in prewar Warsaw; the Germans ordered him to re-form the camp orchestra. From that day the musicians, dressed in tails, played for the SS personnel after each assembly. Changes were also made to the way the assemblies were conducted. After the lists had been checked and all kommandos counted, executions were carried out. Afterwards, the concert began. They always played the Polish song 'Goralu, czy ci nie żal' and 'Fester Schritt', the official anthem of the camp.

In mid-April 1943, the Jewish kommandant Godlewski was replaced by *Kapo* Rakowski, as he was down with an illness, probably typhoid fever, and he could no longer work. Rakowski was a big, tall, broad-shouldered man. It was his physical strength that impressed the Germans. However, he was lenient with his subordinates, while the SS expected him to torture them. The new kommandant introduced a new element into the routine of assemblies – marches. Columns of prisoners marched 'along and across the square'. The Germans thought that this was a way of torturing the prisoners. They were wrong. By means of such exercises, Rakowski and other conspirators hoped to restore the physical strength of the prisoners and in this way prepare them for long marches, in case they succeeded in escaping from the camp.

Unfortunately, Rakowski was not the commander for a long time. Somebody reported to the Germans that he had a flask containing gold in his barracks. His place was searched and following the next assembly he was shot. In the meantime, Engineer Galewski had recovered and the Germans appointed him kommandant again.

It was decided that a zoo would be set up in the camp, and work started on it at the end of April. Two peacocks, a young roe deer and foxes were brought to the camp. The stretch of land around the planned zoo, as well as around the barracks, was dug up and planted with flowers. Franz Stangl himself made the decision to do this. Most of the Jews working in the camp found the idea disgusting.

As the number of transports decreased (now only two trains arrived weekly), the sorting unit became less important. Some groups had already finished work. When the trains were loaded with goods that were to be taken to Germany it turned out that some parcels were missing. The whole sorting unit commanded by *Kapo* Zelo Bloch and *Forarbeiter* Wolf was assigned work in the Treblinka death camp. It was actually a death sentence. In Treblinka II, prisoners working on body disposal were shot dead. Bloch's group was directed to the death camp to replace another group whose members had been liquidated.

After the uprising that broke out in the Warsaw ghetto, transports brought prisoners who had been engaged in the fight. The cars were in a very bad condition; planks of wood had been torn out from them. Many heavily armed guards lay on the roofs ready to fire. During the journey a real battle had been fought with the imprisoned Jews – they knew where they were going and tried desperately to escape from the train. To speed up the whole process of undressing the Germans reorganized things. In addition to the 'Reds', they assigned more prisoners to work and divided them into groups. Each group had to take away different sorts of clothing from the newcomers.

On the first day, while the Jews from the Warsaw ghetto were undressing, there was an explosion. Probably one of them had a grenade hidden in his pocket. Its explosion wounded three prisoners and a few newcomers. All the German officers fled from the square. The Ukrainians and the remaining SS guards surrounded the square. After a few long, silent minutes the Germans recovered from the shock. 'Kiwe' rushed into the square and ordered that the wounded prisoners be taken to the infirmary to be killed. The prisoners did not obey the order, however, they took the wounded out of the square, left them in a barracks adjacent to the platform and laid them on a pile of sorted clothes. 'They [the Germans] pretended not to have noticed that their order had not been obeyed … The whole event was incredible and sensational. It seemed that [the] Germans were afraid of us.'[25]

After the end of April 1943, the Germans no longer selected workers from new transports, and they liquidated all the kommandos that were no longer useful in the camp. During the evening assembly the prisoners who made pots were summoned. This kommando consisted of people between the ages of 40 and 50; people Galewski had selected because they would not be able endure work in other kommandos. Germans arranged them in fives in a line. SS stood all around the square. Josef Hirtieter ordered the prisoners to run. At first they stayed together. Hirtieter ordered them: 'To the ground!' The whole group lay down on the square. SS whipped them where they lay. Then Hirtieter commanded: 'Stand up!' As the prisoners tried to stand the persecutors whipped every part of their bodies, especially the head. Another order was given to run. Covered with blood and dust, they set off. The stronger prisoners ran faster, leaving the weaker ones behind. Hirtieter kept ordering them to lie down and then to stand up. The prisoners were hit constantly by SS. After about half an hour the SS men ordered them to undress. They knew what was about to happen but they were too weak to resist. All of them were shot at the infirmary.

The construction work to modernize and expand the camp continued. Wiernik's unit was responsible for the zoo and the flowerbeds. An additional task was to rebuild the main gate in the Zakopane style; Stangl's quarters were furnished in a similar manner. The floor in the barracks where the SS lived was covered with carpets, in order to muffle the sound of footsteps. A separate building was erected with a container for rainwater on the roof. In a room between two barracks belonging to the SS, arms were stored. The room had a heavy iron door brought to Treblinka especially for this purpose.

At the beginning of May, the Germans found out about Dr Chorazycki's conspiracy activities. Probably a Ukrainian reported on the man. Kurt Franz himself went to Chorazycki to check the information, and he found 700,000 zloty; money which could have been used in case of escape to help Chorazycki to survive. The doctor poisoned himself at the last moment. In this way he spared himself torture and saved many other fellow prisoners who were engaged in the conspiracy.

Outside the camp, the construction of another railway line from Siedlce to Malkinia continued. At the same time the station was adjusted to operate a double-track railway line, and another bridge on the Bug River was built. A building was erected to house the mechanism of the switch block system. Since June 1942, the station had been closed for passenger traffic. An old, wooden building could not be used to regulate the traffic of special trains as it was not good enough to house the switch safety-lock. All railway documents, including the ones that contained information about transports to the extermination camp, were transferred to the new building. From the summer of 1943, the Treblinka railway station was subordinate to the station in Malkinia. Its head was senior superintendent Benner, who often visited the camp and personally supervised the arrival of transports. He was actively involved in the extermination of Jews.

Jews in the camp realized that their existence depended on new transports; they would remain alive as long as new transports arrived. Once the transports stopped stop coming they would become useless to the Germans. Their anxiety mounted when transports from the Warsaw ghetto dried up. The subsequent transports brought less food and money. The workers lived on a starvation diet. The prisoners of camp no. 1 (its administrative part) fed on anything that remained in the storehouses. The prisoners working on body disposal felt the summer heat especially acutely, so the Germans decided that this kommando would work between 4 am and 12 noon. After work Jews were locked in their barracks. Later the Jews worked in shifts: from 12 to 3 pm and from 3 pm to 6 pm. This was their idea (it probably had something to do with the upcoming revolt), and the Germans agreed to it. Food rations were very small; however, the Jews took a certain amount of food from the storehouse and got some from Ukrainians in exchange for other things. With this food the Jews were strong enough to start a revolt.

The Germans seemed composed and relaxed. They often left the camp to bathe in the River Bug.

From the beginning of July, the bodies of those who had been killed in mass executions were brought to the camp and then burnt. Now Germans started trying to obliterate all the traces of extermination. Stones, concrete and other building material were delivered to the camp. It is probable that the camp became a huge crematorium for victims of operational squads:

July was coming to an end. The days were sweltering,

scorching. The hardest work was at the graves, because of the stench … Seventy-five per cent of the victims had already been burnt. Now the ground had to be flattened and the area tidied … The new work started as the empty graves had to be filled up … The empty area had to be used. It was surrounded with a fence of barbed wire. A stretch of land belonging to the other camp was attached. An attempt to plant something in this area was made. The soil turned out to be fertile. The gardeners planted lupin with much success.[26]

In the meantime, the committee responsible for preparing a revolt was ready with a plan and some weapons. They waited for a suitable moment. It was just a matter of time before the Jews in Treblinka would stage an uprising.

NOTES

1. Job 10:20.
2. According to Karol Grunberg, who quotes Wladyslaw Gora, in 1940 Gerstein learned about the circumstances of the death of Bertha Ebling, his sister-in-law, in a mental asylum. He also found out that the same criminal activities were conducted in similar places as a part of the euthanasia programme. He may have decided to disclose the mechanisms of murder to the world. He graduated from a faculty of engineering as well as from a medical school, and consequently he was easily admitted to the SS. He dealt with the problem of fumigation in the concentration and prisoner-of-war camps, constructing a special device for this purpose. Having witnessed the horrifying scenes at the camps when implementing the policy of Operation Reinhard, Gerstein conveyed the information to Baron Goran von Otter, the first secretary of the Swedish Embassy in Berlin, with an order to publish it in the west. K. Grunberg, *Gwardia Hitlera* (Warsaw: PIW, 1994), pp. 414–15.
3. It was never used. The containers were buried on orders of Gerstein on the grounds that they were faulty.
4. Abraham Jakub Krzepicki fought in September 1939. He was taken prisoner, and then released. He settled in Warsaw. On 25 August 1942, he was deported to the extermination camp in Treblinka, from which he managed to flee 18 days later. Afterwards, he went back to Warsaw, where he got in touch with the Jewish Fighting Organization. At the request of Emanuel Ringelblum, Rachela Auerbach wrote down Krzepicki's testimony between December 1942 and January 1943. It was the first known report from Treblinka. Krzepicki himself took part in the Warsaw ghetto uprising in April 1943. Wounded in the leg, he was abandoned by his fellows, like many other wounded soldiers of the Jewish Fighting Organization. They were left in the ruins of the burning buildings. The manuscript of his testimony, recorded in Yiddish and concealed (in a similar way to the whole of Ringelblum's archive), was buried in the ruins of the ghetto. It was found only in December 1950, during excavations at the ruins of the building at 68 Nowolipki Street.
5. Krzepicki, '18 dni w Treblince', pp. 97–8.
6. Blatt, *Sobibor: The Forgotten Revolt*, p. 19.

7. The poisonous gas escaped to the upper parts of the chamber and because of that small children near the floor did not suffocate.
8. Literally: 'Jews' end is ready'.
9. J. Wiernik, *Rok w Treblince, Komisja Koordynacyjna* (Warsaw, 1944), pp. 8–9.
10. The Warsaw ghetto was established on 6 September 1942.
11. He was killed with spades by Ukrainians
12. Max Bialas probably died on the way to the military hospital in Ostrow.
13. Krzepicki, '18 dni w Treblince', p. 109.
14. Excerpts from the verdict passed by the court in Düsseldorf referring to the number of people murdered in Treblinka extermination camp used in indictment against Kurt Franz and nine other members of the camp personnel; ibid., p. 296.
15. Samuel Rajzman was born in Wegrow in 1902. Before the outbreak of war he lived with his wife and young daughter in Warsaw. On 21 September 1942, he was deported to Treblinka. His wife, daughter, two brothers and a sister died. Altogether, 70 members of his family died in the war. During the uprising he was one of the most active participants. His testimony was published in 1944 in a weekly, *Odrodzenie (Revival)*. He was the only witness of the Treblinka camp at the Nuremberg Trials; he was also the main witness at the trails in Düsseldorf and Fort Lauderdale.
16. A quote from Samuel Rajzman's report, *Koniec Treblinki*, quoted from the collection by A. Donat entitled *Death Camp Treblinka: Documentation*, pp. 233–4.
17. The name comes from stable stalls, which were used to build this storehouse.
18. Willenberg, *Bunt w Treblince*, pp. 45–6.
19. Treblinka was visited by Himmler in the spring of 1943.
20. German: 'To Bialystok and Wolkowisko'.
21. Wiernik, *Rok w Treblince*, p. 13.
22. Willenberg, *Bunt w Treblince*, p. 35.
23. Wiernik, *Rok w Treblince*, p. 14.
24. Willenberg, *Bunt w Treblince*, pp. 54–5.
25. Ibid., pp. 54–5.
26. Wiernik, *Rok w Treblince*, p. 19.

6 • *The Conspiracy and Uprising*

The lion tore enough for his cubs, killed enough for his lionesses, and filled his lairs with prey and his dens with torn flesh.[1]

THE ORIGIN OF THE UPRISING

In spite of the horrendous camp conditions, the executions, debilitating work, daily beatings, and the prospect of the extermination of their entire nation, a group of prisoners emerged who were able to survive. These people, thanks to their uncommon strength of character and steadfast will to fight for each day of their lives, managed in time to form a group whose primary goal was to help their fellow prisoners in every possible situation, and thus to save as many people as possible. Those who were saved joined the conspiracy to create a deeply rooted secret organization encompassing every domain of life in the camp. Their ultimate goal, however, which remained in the sphere of dreams especially in the first stages of the camp's operation, was to organize a military rebellion and break out of the camp.

When the conspiracy activities at Treblinka are described, the first thing that needs to be stated is that practically every prisoner in that camp was a conspirator to a greater or lesser degree. It was necessary in the macabre reality in which they had to live.

In the first phase of the history of the camp, it was impossible to conduct any activities that were contrary to the orders of the Germans. The frequent 'exchange' of the work groups was not conducive to conspiracy. If they managed to stay alive, prisoners would confide their thoughts only to their closest colleagues, usually from the neighbouring bunk. Everyone was concentrating on surviving for just another day. There were cases of denunciation among the Jews, and people were very cautious in their contacts with unknown newcomers.

In a sense, it was precisely the cases of denunciation of fellow prisoners and the inhuman conditions which cemented the relationships among people. The links that tied the Jewish workers together were the feelings of shared injustice, the lack of hope for help from outside, and the desire for revenge. As time went by, when there were fewer transports and the composition of the kommandos stabilized, prisoners got to know and trust more of their fellow prisoners. Thus a chain of trust was slowly created, which gave birth to a conspiracy organization within the camp. The heart of that group was formed by the oldest and most experienced prisoners, such as Zev Kurland, or Engineer Galewski, both of whom the Germans and the Ukrainians trusted to a considerable degree.

These people used their positions in the camp hierarchy to help other prisoners. Engineer Galewski, who was the Jewish kommandant of the camp, played a significant role, and therefore had the right to give his opinions on who should be assigned to which work team. In that way he saved lives of many people destined for death. Galewski tirelessly defended prisoners, frequently risking his own life. There were often cases where camp informers were put to death in case they incriminated other prisoners.

A witness, Samuel Willenberg, recalled the case of a Zionist newspaper journalist from Lvov, named Kronenberg, who during the typhoid epidemics was transferred to the fur warehouse[2] at Galewski's suggestion. The journalist was informed of the plans for revolt, although they kept changing every day either as a result of liquidation of the Jews (some of whom had specific tasks to carry out during the uprising) by the Germans, or due to other circumstances, such as installation of additional machine-gun nests. Kronenberg was one of the first conspirators – Galewski chose him personally, and therefore all the Jews trusted him implicitly. Sick and wasted by fever, he lay on a huge pile of furs under mindful care of other prisoners together with others who were also sick.

One day Mitte, an SS, visited the barracks. He saw Kronenberg and, with an ironic smile, asked him tenderly whether he was not sick by any chance. Then he laughed and pushed Kronenberg through the exit towards the infirmary. Kronenberg had been severely weakened by the disease; he stumbled towards the infirmary. Galewski ordered Willenberg to follow the two men. He grabbed a sheet containing trash and ran towards the infirmary.[3] He came down to the pile of burning bodies and tossed the trash on it so that it burned better. Mitte, with his victim, was already in the infirmary. Together with *Kapo* Kurland they stripped Kronenberg of his clothes and pushed him on to the platform above the ditch.

A Ukrainian guard came out of his outhouse. One of the men standing around pushed Kronenberg to the verge of the ramp. The *wachmann* took his gun and reloaded it – preparing to shoot. Kronenberg started shouting in German: 'I want to live, I will help you, and I will tell you everything. There is a conspiracy here. A hundred people belong to it.' The Ukrainian *wachmann*, not understanding what was said, wanted to save Mitte from Kronenberg's grip. He shot him in the head.[4]

The organizer of the plot at Treblinka was Dr Julian Chorazycki; though the name of a Czech Jew, Rudolf Masarek,[5] is mentioned equally often in this connection. Both of them were soldiers – Chorazycki had been a captain in the Polish Army and a prominent Warsaw laryngologist; while Masarek had been a captain in the Czech Army before the outbreak of the war. They were the initiators of the uprising. Chorazycki persuaded Engineer Galewski to participate, and thus Galewski became one of the key figures in the conspiracy. Many people joined in, but the organization committee was limited to 12 persons. Samuel Rajzman recalls that:

> We had four companies, each of 12 people, the total of about 50 persons ready for action … Every participating person knew just one member of the committee. The point was to avoid the situation, in which one captured participant who would be tortured by the Germans could reveal the name of more than one other person involved in the uprising.[6]

Since members of the organizing committee were not able to meet freely, it was established that they would meet in the Strawaczynscy brothers' car body shop or the carpenters' workshop. The meetings took place at night and the participants pretended that they were playing cards. Card games were officially banned so prisoners had to sneak out at night to play, but the worst punishment for the players was a mere 20 lashes. According to Rajzman, the uprising committee had already been formed by October 1942.

In planning the uprising, the Jews obviously had to take into account the weapons of the German and Ukrainian guards. Against the pistols, automatic guns, rifles and grenades, the conspirators could only put up blunt knives,[7] spades and hammers. The first issue then was that of weapons. There were two possibilities – theft from the camp arsenal, or purchase of weapons from the local villagers through the mediation of the Ukrainians. The only way to reach the arsenal weapons was to steal the key, which was a mission impossible. In the arsenal there were a few Finnish automatic guns with ammunition, and German hand grenades. They were stored there in case of the 'loss of control' over a new transport. The entrance to the building was carefully guarded by Ukrainian patrols and had a heavy iron door; the key to which was in the hands of the Germans.

A camp locksmith had fitted the lock to the door but because he was under guard while doing his job, he was unable to make a copy of the key at that time. Several dramatic weeks passed by. Finally, a happy coincidence helped the prisoners when the lock became broken and the locksmith called to repair it was able to make a wax copy this time. It took several weeks to make a duplicate key due to the lack of adequate material and the complexity of the lock.

At last, having free access to the arsenal, the organizing committee decided to ask the Jewish boys who worked for the SS for help. The boys were young, aged between 13 and 15, and they cleaned the barracks, ironed uniforms and shirts, cleaned shoes, etc. In exchange, they received food and they were free to move around the camp. One of them was sent to the arsenal with the key in order to find out what was there. The boy returned with a hand grenade, which unfortunately did not have a fuse. He described the weapons hanging on a wooden rack and boxes with grenades. Masarek, Chorazycki and Galewski made a decision that the boy should go there again. It still took several weeks; in the meantime Chorazycki was killed while trying to arrange another source of weapons. Finally, the boy returned with a grenade and several guns. They were hidden in a potato cellar. Since all plans had failed until then, it was necessary to come up with a new plan that could be implemented.

Instead of the lost 'Flaschensortiren kommando', Engineer Galewski proposed to the Germans that one prisoner be selected to pick up trash throughout the whole camp. It was a welcome proposal as far as the Germans were concerned because the Ukrainians kept dropping food remnants, bottles, etc., everywhere, completely ignoring the white-painted barrels placed for that purpose. Galewski got permission for this move, and from then on a prisoner named Alfred – a member of the conspiracy – was given the right to move around the camp freely in search of trash. He was to become a liaison between the boys working at the SS barracks and the rest of the camp.

The plan for the uprising was not complicated. The Germans were in the habit of leaving the camp periodically in groups of two to three to visit their families in Germany. In addition, on hot summer days, most of the camp staff would cycle to the nearby River Bug for a swim. Only a handful of Ukrainians on duty and several SS men stayed in the camp. The rate of desertion among the *wachmanns* had been high for some time, which indicated that their morale was low. Ukrainian escapes were brought on by German defeats at the Eastern Front and their fear that they would all be executed when the camp was closed so as to obliterate all traces of its activities. Taking advantage of the absence of many of the staff, with the help of the boys it was possible to steal the weapons from the SS arsenal and hide them either in a potato cellar or in piles of potatoes lying on the other side of the road. From there, weapons could be distributed to the prisoners by the boys, who wandered about the camp all the time so nobody was suspicious of them. In the Zaunkommando barracks there were tools for cutting wire and working wood (pliers, axes, shears, hammers, etc.) which could be used as weapons, and then to cut a way through the fence. Every member of the conspiracy was supposed to be issued with poison in the event of capture and enough money and gold to survive outside.

On the day of the revolt, after distributing the weapons, the Jewish boys were to throw grenades at the SS buildings. The prisoners who maintained the German cars were to pour gasoline on them and set them on fire. The construction kommando got the task of seizing the armoured vehicle and opening the main gate of the camp. Another group was to cut the telephone lines, and yet another one was to remove the Ukrainian guards on the watch towers. Those who had not been issued with weapons were to destroy all buildings and to kill every member of the camp staff they possibly could. Having carried out their tasks all inmates were to run to the forest and try to save themselves.

There were 12 people in each of the four groups of conspirators, and the number of prisoners staying at the camp at that time is estimated to have been 1,200. According to the plans for the uprising, all members of the conspiracy groups (about 50 people in all) were to receive weapons, which unfortunately turned out to be impossible.

The plan had two essential disadvantages: it did not take into consideration the stage of preparations for the uprising in camp no. 2, and it did not take into account the fact that the smoke from the burning barracks and the sounds of gunfire could alarm the staff of the labour camp Treblinka I, which had telephone connection with all garrisons in the vicinity. In spite of this, the decision was made to go ahead with the uprising. It was accelerated by the secret construction work involving the newly arrived building materials – according to witness accounts, the Germans were building new grates.[8]

The last question was the date of the beginning of the revolt. The workers from camp no. 2 still did not know when and at what time the rebellion was to start. After much hesitation, it was determined for Monday, 2 August, at 16.45. The reasons for selecting that hour are given by Rajzman:

> At five o'clock, our camp was passed by a train carrying workers from the second Treblinka.[9] We decided that we could stop that train at five – it always carried 200 to 300 people coming back from work. We would free those people from the train and they would help us in the uprising.[10]

The signal to start the revolt was to be a single shot from a pistol.

The date was determined four days in advance. From Friday, the Jewish crew prepared for the uprising by digging out the knives and money hidden underground, and organizing the groups. On Sunday, 1 August 1943, around noon, the last consultations among the group leaders took place. They were given the pistols acquired by means of trade. It was decided that Wiernik, together with a few helpers, would find a pretext to go down to camp no. 1 and personally find out at what time the uprising was to break out. Everything seemed to be ready.

THE COURSE OF THE UPRISING ON 2 AUGUST 1943

On Monday, 2 August, an atmosphere of tension could be felt from early on. Perhaps the Germans sensed it too. Rajzman recalls that one of the SS saw two boys saying goodbye to each other, and one Jew standing and weeping, so he demanded an explanation from Galewski. The latter fobbed him off with some lies, but, realizing the impossibility of concealing the preparations any longer, around noon he gave the order to capture some weapons. As a result of burglary carried out by Jacek (a boy from Hungary) and Jakub Miller, it was possible to seize two boxes of grenades – about 80 pieces in total – and 37 guns and pistols. They were hidden in a cart and taken to the rubbish dump.

At the last moment it turned out that the grenades were missing fuses. Fortunately, the boy managed to fetch them within 15 minutes. The nerves of the conspirators were stretched to the limit.

A certain Rudek from Plock distributed the weapons. He asked everyone who came to give the password; the password was 'Death' and the response was 'Life'.

A very important role was played by prisoner of about 25 or 26 by the name of Bendin, whose job was the disinfection of clothes. Around 3 o'clock, he was walking through the camp as usual, but instead of the usual disinfectant he poured flammable liquid stolen from the parking lot round each of the barracks.

In the early afternoon, Kurt Franz, in the company of several SS and 16 Ukrainians, went to the River Bug to take a swim.

Unfortunately, the Jewish conspirators did not manage to start the uprising as scheduled: a few minutes before 4 pm 'Kiewe'[11] came up to a boy who was standing with stuffed pockets. He seized him and pulled money from his pockets. He showered the boy with an avalanche of invective. During this incident another Jew approached. Kiewe took both of them (the man and the boy) behind the barracks and started to beat them mercilessly.

The planned hour had not yet come, but they were afraid that Kiewe's victims might break down and confess, resulting in the capture of all the conspirators. There was no alternative but to take up arms immediately:

One of us went to the window and shot at 'Kiewe' with a pistol. 'Kiewe' died on the spot.[12] Exactly a minute later

Franz Suchomel appeared on his bicycle. He was also shot at, but inaccurately, and he responded with fire. We ran out of the barracks, we cut the telephone cables, and set fire to the warehouse and the barracks, on which we had poured gasoline on an hour before.[13]

At the same time, in camp no. 2, Captain Zelo Bloch attacked two SS guards with an axe, and joined the uprising with a group of prisoners. Rudek, who has already been mentioned, managed to take control of an armoured vehicle and opened fire at the Germans. The rest of the weapons were distributed from the arsenal; those who did not get weapons grabbed shovels and axes. The barracks were burning, the gas chamber building was set on fire, and grenades were thrown at the SS barracks. Some of the *wachmanns* escaped, but several died in their watch towers. The remaining ones opened fire at the rebels with their machine-guns. In view of the shortage of munitions, and in fear of the return of the rest of the camp staff, the prisoners cut the fence wires and escaped, leaving the bodies of their compatriots and the burning camp buildings behind.

A large group of the freed Jews went into the forests and crossed the River Bug in the vicinity of Glina village. As it turned out they were covered and helped during the crossing by an AK[14] detachment under the command of Stanislaw Siwek, whose pseudonym was Sliwa:

The whole vicinity was alarmed immediately[15] ... Bahnschütze, army, gendarmerie from Kosow Lacki, Sokolow Podlaski, Ostrowek, Malkinia, Ostrow Mazowiecka, and even the fire brigade from Malkinia called by the Germans, all were going to help the crew of the camp. All roads were blocked.[16]

Most of the Jews did not know the area. They were captured and brutally murdered. The Germans issued an order informing the Polish population that Jews were infected with typhus and that helping them in any way would be punished by death. In spite of this order, many Poles gave shelter to the Jews so that later under cover of darkness they could be led, or pointed, in a safe direction.

The witnesses say that there were also cases of Jews who gave up on the escape, and after several days of wandering returned to the camp and gave themselves up voluntarily to death, so they could be where their families had gone.

The fugitives were chased not only by the German units; the Polish police were also included in the operation. All garrisons from Malkinia to Siedlce were mobilized. Houses, barns, buildings, rail cars were searched; the woods and meadows in the vicinity were combed with tracker dogs. The fugitives were recognizable from a distance: they were Jews with shaved heads. In railway stations and other public places there were posters warning of the escape of 50 Jewish bandits. People were warned not to hide them because they carried typhus.

Some Polish peasants helped the escapees, but there were also cases of refusal of help, usually caused by fear of German repression. There were also hideous cases of denouncement of the fugitives as so-called *szmalcownictwo*.[17]

Although the posters mentioned only 50 bandits, in fact the main result of the uprising was the escape of about 200 prisoners; moreover, as a result of the rebellion, several barracks were burned down and more than a dozen camp staff members killed; all of whom, interestingly enough, were Ukrainians. The total destruction of the camp was not achieved, and despite the damage, within a few days of the uprising it began to receive new transports of victims. Out of the 200 fugitives, probably around 87 survived, although the number may be exaggerated.

The revolt in Treblinka caused serious confusion among the staff of Operation Reinhard in Lublin. The immediate liquidation of the camp was considered. No report of the uprising was sent to the T4 headquarters in Berlin. Apparently, Globocnik decided that since there had been no casualties among the SS the camp could continue to function, and there was no reason to disturb Himmler.

Less than a week after the rebellion, there was a change in camp kommandant – SS-Hauptsturmführer Franz Stangl was superseded by his deputy Kurt Franz, now promoted to the rank of SS-Untersturmführer. He was to continue the work of his predecessor until the liquidation of the camp. Stangl was transferred to northern Italy (near Trieste) where he was to realize his 'commanding talents' in relation to the local population.

2 AUGUST–NOVEMBER 1943

When they rushed back to the camp from their trip to the river, the SS and the Ukrainians saw the unburned remnants of the barracks, the smouldering SS barracks,[18] the gas chamber building dark with smoke, destroyed fences, warehouses, 'railway station' installations, dead bodies of Jews and Ukrainians, and the wounded Küttner (Kiewe). The losses on the German side were relatively small – one wounded German and about six Ukrainians dead or wounded. Not all of the Jews escaped – out of about 600, 100 remained in the camp – those were the sick, the emaciated, or the ones who had simply failed escape; about 400 of them died in the camp or in its immediate surroundings; and an unspecified number were killed by the pursuing Germans. It is estimated that only around 100 prisoners succeeded in breaking out of the hell that was Treblinka II on 2 August 1943.

The first days after the rebellion were devoted to putting out the fires and cleaning the camp. The work was supervised personally by Stangl, and after his departure, by the new kommandant Kurt Franz. The prisoners of the labour camp Treblinka I were used to put the camp compound in order; 100 of them were sent to the site by the order of Kommandant van Euppen. No efforts were made to restore the camp to the condition it was in before the uprising. The burned down barracks were not reconstructed; the objective was simply to clean the area and provisionally prepare the camp to receive new transports.

According to the testimony of Franciszek Zabecki, the following transports arrived at or passed the station in Treblinka in August 1943:

18 August – transport 'PJ-201' with 32 wagons passed through Treblinka to Lublin

18 August – transport 'PJ-202' with 37 wagons arrived at the extermination camp Treblinka II from Bialystok

19 August – transport 'PJ-203' with 40 wagons passed through Treblinka to Lublin

19 August – transport 'PJ-204' with 39 wagons arrived at the extermination camp Treblinka II from Bialystok

24 August – transport 'PJ-209' with 9 wagons passed through Treblinka to Lublin

8 September – transport 'PJ-211' with 31 wagons passed through Treblinka to Lublin

17 September – transport 'PJ-1025' with 50 wagons passed through Treblinka from Minsk to Chelm.[19]

The last train carrying 'deportees' arrived at the Treblinka II camp on 19 August 1943. Both the last transport and the preceeding one (18 August) were received in a slightly different way than the ones before the uprising. A switching engine detached ten (instead of 20) wagons from the train waiting at the station, and pushed them towards the death camp. The reason was that there were now fewer personnel at Treblinka II and a smaller number of prisoners employed to sort the clothes.

After the final 19 August transport, things quietened down at the camp. On that day the last Jews brought to Treblinka were gassed. More and more trains were directed south, to Lublin. After 19 August, all 'special' trains bypassed the death camp in Treblinka and went on to Majdanek and Sobibor.

Upon completion of the liquidation of the ghetto in Bialystok, Operation Reinhard was also wound up. In recognition of his 'achievements', Odilo Globocnik was promoted by Himmler and got the position of the Higher SS and Police Kommandant in Trieste. Together with Wirth, Stangl and other participants in the Operation (including the Ukrainians), left Lublin in September 1943 and went to northern Italy.

Starting on 22 August, single wagons loaded with the sorted clothes of the murdered victims were dispatched from the death camp. They were attached to other trains waiting at the Treblinka station. Zabecki states that:

> Such wagons left the camp on 2, 9, 13 and 21 September.[20] … On 30 September, the German railwayman, Rudolf Emmerich, who was employed to watch the transports entering the death camp, left the Treblinka station and went to Warsaw. At the beginning of October, it was noticed at the station in Treblinka that elements of disassembled barracks, wooden planks, chlorinated lime … were being shipped out of the death camp. Later, the digger-dredger machine which was no longer needed was taken away.[21]

The remnants of the camp were removed with great attention to detail. The barbed wire from the fence was wound up and taken to the work camp Treblinka I, together with the anti-tank 'stacks'. Both buildings containing the gas chambers were pulled down. On 20 October a transport of four cargo wagons 'Nos 22757, 130789, 22536, 70136' left the camp.[22] It was headed for the death camp in Sobibor. The contents were officially registered as *Häftlinge* – prisoners.[23]

> A similar transport left on 4 November, also to Sobibor – this time it consisted of three wagons with Jewish workers. On 21 October, the engines of the gas chambers and all other iron materials were sent out, probably to Lublin. On 5 November, the armoured vehicle serving formerly to transport valuables was shipped out. Trains throughout the whole of October 1943 and part of November 1943 shipped out planks, bricks, rubble and all other construction materials. … since the beginning of the liquidation until 17 November 1943, over 100 wagons of equipment were sent out.[24]

On 17 November, the last Ukrainian *wachmanns* left for Lublin. Shortly thereafter, at Kurt Franz's request, one of the SS took the dog Bari to his friend, the manager of a hospital in Ostrow.

All traces of the activities of the former camp were removed or destroyed. The land was ploughed, levelled and sowed with lupins. A small house and farm buildings were built from the remnants of the construction materials. A former *wachmann* by the name of Strebel was to move in there, together with his whole family from the Ukraine. His mission was to keep an eye on the land covered by the former camp. In case of any questions, he was to maintain that he had lived there for many years.

However, before Strebel managed to move in, the last execution took place on the camp grounds. In the second half of November 1943, apart from the few SS (kommandant Kurt Franz among them), just 25 or 30 Jewish prisoners remained, living in two railway wagons. Among them were two women working in the kitchen of the previously mentioned farm. On, or about, 16 November, an order came from Lublin to withdraw from Treblinka, and put to death all of the remaining prisoners. Franz carried out the execution as follows: the Jews were locked in the two wagons. Sensing what was awaiting them, one of the prisoners hanged himself. The rest waited quietly for death. With the aid of the Ukrainians borrowed from the work camp, lines of armed men were formed from the wagons to the house of the newly built farm, to prevent the victims escaping. Next, SS-Unterscharführer Bredow went to the kitchen to fetch the two women working there and brought them out. At the same time, five men were let out of the first wagon. The victims had to to kneel down in a small area of lower ground to the left of the house and bow their heads. Willy Mentz, Paul Bredow and an SS-Unterführer (not known by name), commander of the unit of Ukrainians who came from the labour camp, carried out the executions. The three of them stood behind the seven kneeling prisoners. One shot the two victims on the left in the neck, the next one shot the three in the middle, and the third one finished off the two on the right. After the first group had been murdered the next five men were led out, and they had to carry the still warm bodies of the killed ones to the stake prepared earlier by the Ukrainians, and then kneel down with their heads bowed where those killed before them had knelt. This is how the last prisoners of Treblinka were shot. When the last five were dead, the Ukrainians threw their bodies on the pile. Their task was also to make sure that the victims were completely burned and to remove all traces of the pyre. Immediately after the executions, Kurt Franz, together with Mentz and Bredow, said goodbye to the SS-Unterführer from Treblinka I and left for Sobibor by truck.[25]

NOTES

1. Nahum 2:12.
2. The Germans assumed that lice were breeding in the warm warehouse, so they avoided the building.
3. The infirmary was not only the place of mass shootings, but also the place where large quantities of trash were burned.
4. Willenberg, *Bunt w Treblince*, pp. 39–40.
5. Rudolf Masarek – a Czech Jew (actually a half-Jew; his wife was a Jew). After the transfer of Zhelomir Bloch to camp no. 2, he took over the military command of the underground organization. Masarek played one of the main roles in the uprising. Some witnesses mistakenly write his name as 'Masaryk', which gave rise to the myth that the man was presumably somehow related to the first president of Czechoslovakia – Thomas Masaryk. As a matter of fact, Masarek's family had a shop selling smart shirts in Prague, and Rudolf Masarek himself came to Treblinka because he was accompanying his wife, who was arrested and deported to Terezin and then to Treblinka.
6. S. Rajzman, *The End of Treblinka*, from the collection edited by Donat, *Death Camp Treblinka*, p. 242.
7. After the murder of Max Bielas, the Jews were not allowed to carry, or to use at

work, knives with sharp points. On Stangl's order, all knives had to have rounded points.

8. Grinberg, *The Revolt in Treblinka*, from Donat, *Death Camp Treblinka*, p. 219.
9. A work camp situated two kilometres from the death camp.
10. Rajzman, *The End of Treblinka*, p. 243.
11. Oberscharführer Kurt Küttner.
12. Küttner was only wounded. He died after the war.
13. Grinberg, *The Revolt in Treblinka*, from Donat, *Death Camp Treblinka*, p. 221.
14. The Polish Home Army.
15. Seeing the smoke rising over the death camp, the Germans from the neighbouring penal camp ran to the nearest SIPo HQ to raise the alarm.
16. F. Zabecki, *Wspomnienia dawne i nowe* (Warsaw: PAX, 1977), pp. 94–5.
17. There is no English equivalent for this word, which describes the selling of the Jews to the Germans by the Poles.
18. The camp burned until 18.00 hours.
19. Zabecki, *Wspomnienia dawne i nowe*, pp. 96–8.
20. Witnesses attested that the works related to the liquidation of the camp were started towards the end of September 1943.
21. Zabecki, *Wspomnienia dawne i nowe*, pp. 97–8.
22. Ibid., pp. 98–9.
23. It was made up of prisoners working at the disassembly, who were no longer needed.
24. Zabecki, *Wspomnienia dawne i nowe*, p. 99.
25. The report about the execution was taken from 'excerpts from judgements (*urteilsbegründung*) against Kurt Franz and nine members of the Treblinka personnel on September 3, 1965', and other material from Franz Stangl's trial before a Düsseldorf court on 22 December 1970, from Donat, *Death Camp Treblinka*, pp. 315–16.

7 • *The Body Count*

*For behold, the Lord is about to come out from His place
To punish the inhabitants of the earth for their iniquity;
And the earth will reveal her bloodshed,
And will no longer cover her slain.*[1]

A SUMMARY OF ACTIVITIES AT TREBLINKA II

Treblinka II operated from 23 July 1942 until 19 August 1943.[2] Based on the differing numbers of incoming transports, that 13-month period should be divided into five stages:

- From 23 June until the middle of December 1942. At that time, the camp was receiving two to three transports daily, excluding holidays, when no trains arrived; thus, we can assume an average of two transports per day as a reliable number.
- From 15 December 1942 until 15 January 1943. It is assumed that at that time the camp received one transport per week, i.e. four transports in total.
- From 15 January until the end of May 1943. The camp was receiving two transports per week on average.
- From May until 2 August 1943. There was one transport per week on average.
- From 2 August until 19 August 1943. There were two transports.

It is very difficult to establish the precise number of transports that arrived at Treblinka, because most of the German railway documents (telegrams, timetables) were destroyed on purpose to remove the evidence. As a result of the mass burning of the victims and the liquidation of the graves in the camp, it is impossible to determine the exact number of victims of Treblinka. On the basis of the available information (witnesses' testimonies, shipping documents) we are in a position to calculate approximately how many persons' ashes rest in the soil of the former extermination camp.

99

The mechanism of calculation of an approximate number of victims is as follows.

Assuming that each railway wagon from Poland held an average of 120 persons and that the passenger cars (for those travelling from the western European countries) held an average of 30 persons, and also that all of the Polish trains had an average of 45 wagons (and trains from Western Europe, an averge of 20 wagons), we can estimate that there were about 5,400 people per transport arriving from the Government General, or the so-called 'Eastern Territories'; and about 600 people per transport arriving from western (and southern) Europe.

Now we have to multiply the average daily number of transports by the number of days per month when the camp was operating. That will enable us to obtain the monthly average of transports coming in; and the sum of those numbers from all periods will show us the approximate number of transports which arrived at the camp during the whole period of its operation. When we multiply that number by the relevant values denoting the number of people in a given transport (domestic or foreign), we will obtain the approximate number of victims in Treblinka. The number of people in the domestic and foreign wagons should be averaged out, which will give the result of 3,000 in one transport (i.e. 100 persons per wagon). It must be noted that, when calculating the number of days when the camp was operating, holidays, Sundays and camp visitation days should be excluded, because transports did not arrive on those days.

Having made the calculations described above, in relation to the specific periods of functioning of the camp, we arrive at the following numbers:

- From 23 June until 15 December 1942 the camp operated for 120 days, during which time there were approximately 240 transports, which gives the result of 720,000 victims.
- From 15 December 1942 until 15 January 1943 there were four transports and about 12,000 people died.
- From 15 January until the end of May 1943 there were 36 transports and about 108,000 people died.
- From the end of May until 2 August 1943 there were eight transports and about 24,000 people died.
- From 2 August until 19 August 1943 there were two transports

and about 6,000 people died (this number includes about 550 Jews killed during the uprising).

One has to bear in mind that these numbers do not include the transports arriving at Treblinka by means other than rail. The data also do not include the prisoners who worked both on the construction of the camp (approximately 1,000) and at its liquidation (100 to 200 prisoners).

Thus, on the basis of the calculation above, taking into account also those who died during the construction and liquidation of the camp, we can assume that approximately 870,000 people died in the Treblinka II extermination camp.

Other publications give figures ranging from 700,000[3] (the account by Dr Helmut Krusnick, director of the Institute of History in Munich, appointed to be the expert witness at the trial of the crew of Treblinka in Dusseldorf on 3 September 1965) to three million victims.[4] The calculations made by different authors, the accounts by witnesses concerning the frequency of transports (especially in the last days of the camp preceding the uprising), as well as the methods used, are often contradictory. On the one hand, it seems understandable considering the incomplete documentation and witness accounts; and, on the other, it confronts a young researcher of the history of the camp with the bitter awareness of dealing with information which is not thoroughly proven, or which is unclear.

THE FATE OF THE OPPRESSORS

They shall become repulsive carrion and eternal laughing stock among the dead.[5]

Odilo Globocnik – born on 21 April 1904, in Trieste, SS-Brigadeführer, chief of Operation Reinhard, SS and police kommandant in the Lublin district. All dedicated extermination camps were under his command. During Himmler's visit to the Warsaw ghetto, he personally supervised his security. In his report after the completion of Operation Reinhard, he estimated the value of the stolen property to be 178 million Reichsmarks. Having finished operations in Polish territory, he was sent to northern Italy to fight the guerrillas there. Based in Trieste, he was awarded the post of a Higher SS and Police Kommandant. The people who found themselves under his command in Italy were the same people who had made up the personnel of the extermination camps in Poland. They were sent to fight the guerrillas with full awareness that their Yugoslav opponents did not take any prisoners. Having fled his native Trieste to escape the approaching Allied forces, Globocnik went to Carinthia where British soldiers arrested him. Soon thereafter, he committed suicide at the prison in Weissensee, on 21 May 1945.

Victor Brack – SS-Oberführer, chief of the 2nd Department at Hitler's office responsible for the T4 operation that resulted in the death of approximately 50,000 disabled Germans and Jews. Parallel to the preparations for the 'Final Solution', in the summer of 1941 he conducted research into the mass sterilization of the Jews by means of X-rays. He was responsible for the personnel assigned to Operation Reinhard on behalf of Hitler's office. After the war, he was one of the main defendants at the so-called 'Trial of the Physicians' in Nuremberg. In 1947, the American Military Tribunal sentenced Brack to death by hanging. The sentence was carried out one year later.

Christian Wirth – SS-Sturmbannführer, the inspector of the Operation Reinhard camps, their creator, and the first kommandant of Chelmno and Belzec. In the autumn of 1943 he received the order to supervise the liquidation of the death camps. After having accomplished that, he was promoted to the rank of SS-Sturmbannführer, and subsequently – like other members assigned to Operation Reinhard by Hitler's office – he was sent to northern Italy to fight the uprising there. He was killed in an ambush organized by the Yugoslav guerrillas on the road to Fiume, near Trieste, on 26 May 1944.

Dr Irmfired Eberl – we know relatively little about this physician-kommandant of an extermination camp. After having been removed from the post of kommandant of Treblinka, he did not receive any other assignment. He committed suicide in 1948.

Franz Paul Stangl – born on 26 March 1908. He was kommandant of the camps in Sobibor and Treblinka with the rank of SS-Hauptsturmführer. After the uprising in Treblinka he supervised the workers clearing the damage for a few days, and he was subsequently transferred to the vicinity of Trieste to fight the guerrillas. Contrary to the expectations of the authors of the transfer, he survived and returned to his native Austria after the war. There, amidst the surge of arrests of the members of the prewar T4 team, he was arrested for his activities in Hartheim. He escaped from prison and went to Italy. Thanks to the help of Bishop Alois Hudal (within the Deliverance Action conducted by the Vatican), using the diplomatic passport issued to him by the Vatican, he went to Syria, where he lived for some time. In 1951, he moved with his family to Brazil. There he found a job initially at a textile factory, and later at the Volkswagen factory in Sao Paulo. In Brazil he lived under his own name and used his Austrian passport. In the mid-1960s, the famous Nazi hunter Simon Wiesenthal received an offer from an anonymous informer to identify Stangl. In return he demanded 'one cent for each Jew killed in Treblinka', i.e. $7,000. Stangl was arrested by the Brazilian police. On 23 June 1967, he was sent to Germany – because the condition for his extradition was that he should be tried in a German court. The trial started on 22 May 1970, and it ended with Stangl receiving a sentence of life imprisonment on 22 December 1970. While awaiting the hearing of his appeal, he died suddenly of a stroke on 28 June 1971.

Karl Hubert Franz – 'The Doll', born in 1914 in Düsseldorf. SS-Untersturmführer, member of the crew of Sobibor, the last kommandant of the camp in Treblinka, he supervised its liquidation. He fulfilled the same function in dismantling the camp in Sobibor. In late autumn 1943, he was transferred to the area of Trieste to fight the guerrillas. After the war he did not take advantage of the help from the Vatican and he returned to his native Düsseldorf, where he even applied for a name change. He was only arrested on 2 December 1959. On that day, during the search of his apartment, an album was found which contained several photos from Treblinka: pictures of Stangl, camp views, pictures of the dog Bari, the dredging machines for digging pits for corpses, etc. The album was entitled 'The best years of my life'.[6] He was tried together with nine other members of the camp personnel in a trial in Düsseldorf, which began on 12 October 1964 and ended on 3 September 1965. Karl Hubert Franz was sentenced to hard labour for life. Due to his age, he was released in May 1993. He lives in Düsseldorf.

Josef Hirtreiter – 'Sepp', member of the camp staff at Treblinka. He was particularly cruel to children; an attribute which is recalled by all witnesses. As with other Treblinka personnel, once he had left the camp he fought the Yugoslav guerrillas. After the war he returned to Germany. He was the first member of the Treblinka crew to be sentenced after the war. On 3 March 1951, a court in Frankfurt sentenced him to life imprisonment.

Kurt Küttner – 'Kiewe' – SS-Scharführer. One of the kommandants of camp no. 1 at the Treblinka II extermination compound. Personally supervised the arrival of each transport. Wounded during the uprising, he died in Germany shortly after the war.

Otto Richard Horn – SS-Unterscharführer, worked as an operator of a digging machine. Quiet; compassionate to Jews going to their death. After the war he remained in Germany. He was acquitted by the court in Düsseldorf in 1965.

Erwin Lambert – born in 1910, SS-Unterscharführer, the constructor of the gas chambers in Sobibor and Treblinka. He remained in Germany after the war. Sentenced to three years during the trial of the crew of Treblinka in Düsseldorf in 1965.

Arthur Matthes – born in 1902 – SS-Scharführer, one of the kommandants of camp no. 2 at the Treblinka extermination compound. Responsible for the efficient operation of the gas chambers. Sentenced to hard labour for life at the trial of the crew of Treblinka in Düsseldorf in 1965.

Willy Mentz – born in 1904, SS-Unterscharführer, 'Frankenstein', chief of the infirmary in Treblinka. Responsible for the deaths of thousands of victims. He participated in the liquidation of the camp, and in the last execution carried out on its premises. He was sentenced to hard labour for life by the court in Düsseldorf in 1965.

August Miete – born in 1909, SS-Unterscharführer, 'Angel of Death', assistant to Mentz at the infirmary. Like his superior, he was responsible for the deaths of thousands of victims killed in that terrible place. He ruthlessly sought the weaker, older, sick prisoners, children, and pregnant women, both in the camp and in the incoming transports. He was sentenced to hard labour for life by the court in Düsseldorf in 1965.

Gustaw Münzberger – born in 1903, SS-Unterscharführer, assistant to Matthes at camp no. 2 of the Treblinka II compound. Gas chamber operator. He was sentenced to 12 years in prison at the trial in Düsseldorf.

Albert Rum – born in 1890, SS-Unterscharführer, supervised the marching of the victims to the gas chambers at the Treblinka II camp. He was sentenced to three years in prison at the trial in Düsseldorf.

Otto Sadie – born in 1897, SS-Stabsscharführer, responsible for the Ukrainian *wachmanns* in Treblinka. One of the murderers of *Kapo* Rakowski. He was sentenced to six years in prison at the trial in Düsseldorf.

Franz Suchomel – born in 1908, SS-Unterscharführer, chief of the *Goldjuden* kommando in Treblinka. He directly supervised the sorting of money and valuables. He was sentenced to seven years in prison by the court in Düsseldorf.

NOTES

1. Isaiah 26:21.
2. Of all the authors who published material on Treblinka, both in Poland and abroad, it was only Ryszard Czarkowski who claimed (on the basis of his own experience) that the extermination centre was already in operation on 25 June 1942: R. Czarkowski, *Cieniom Treblinki* (Warsaw: Wydawnictwo MON, 1989), pp. 191–2.
3. In his account, Dr Helmu Krausnick showed that during the period from 22 June 1942 to 23 August 1943, more than 700,000 people were killed in Treblinka. From Donat, *Death Camp Treblinka*, pp. 296–7.
4. V. Grosman, *Piekło Treblinki* (Katowice: Wydawnictwo Literatura Polska, 1945), p. 7.
5. Wisdom 4:19.
6. In German, 'Die schönsten Jahre meines Lebens.'

Appendix 1

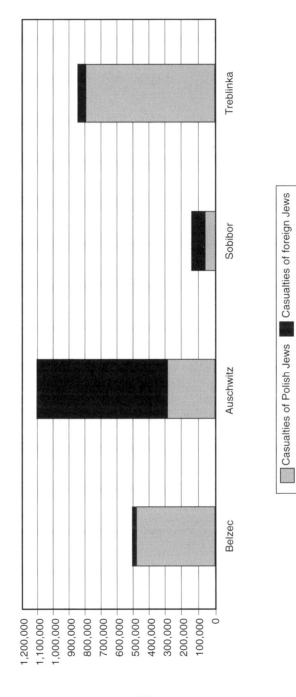

Source: Marszałek, J. *Obozy pracy w Generalnym Gubernatorstvie w latach 1939–1945* (Lublin: Państwowe Muzeum na Majdanku, 1998).

APPENDIX 2
SCHEMATIC DIAGRAM SHOWING OPERATION REINHARD
CHAIN OF COMMAND

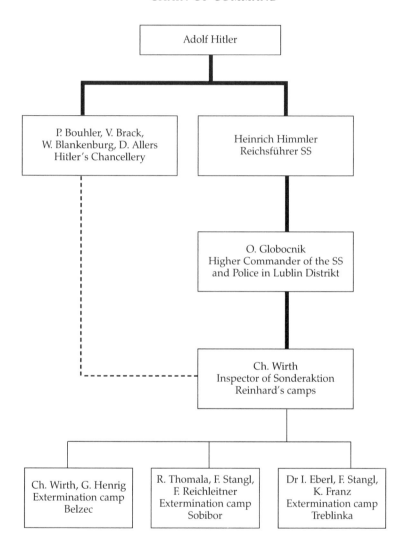

Source: Burba, M. *Treblinka* (Lokheide, 1995), p. 6.

APPENDIX 3
NAZI EXTERMINATION CAMPS IN POLAND

Source: Burba, M. *Treblinka* (Lokheide, 1995), p. 4.

APPENDIX 4
PLAN OF THE EXTERMINATION CAMP TREBLINKA II

Source: Burba, M. *Treblinka* (Lokheide, 1995), p. 7.

Death camp

n with twigs (3-4 m high)

ıngslager

linka

Pit no. 1

Earth embankment

Pit no. 4

Pit no. 2

40-50 m wide
belt of the ground

Pit no. 3

Washing square

New position
of watchtower

Grate

Well

Barrier

Engine

Old
gas
chambers

New

Road to gas chambers (schlauch)

gas chambers

Engine
room

Small
door

Original position
of watchtower
transferred
to the death camp

Women
Doctor
Kapo
Bath
Latrine
Men
Kitchen

Gate

Bottle and pot collecting square

Pit for test burning

Unused pit for bodies

Shift guards

Gate

Barbers

Disinfection

Cash desk

Board

Undressing
room for men

Latrine

Earth embankment

Undressing
room for
women
and children

The Reds

"Lazarett"

Well

Women to the left

Men to the right

Reception camp

Sorting square

Sorting kommando

Burning pit

Ukrainian guardhouse

e Ukrainian guard

l heap

Garage

Station square

Clock

Big sorting barrack (so called "station")

Pit for corpses
from transports

Pay-desk

Gate

The Blues

Ramp

Swing door

Small fence

To the Treblinka I labour camp

ply square

Lazaret

Appendix 5

DRAFT OF THE ORGANIZATION OF DEPORTATIONS TO
EXTERMINATION CAMPS

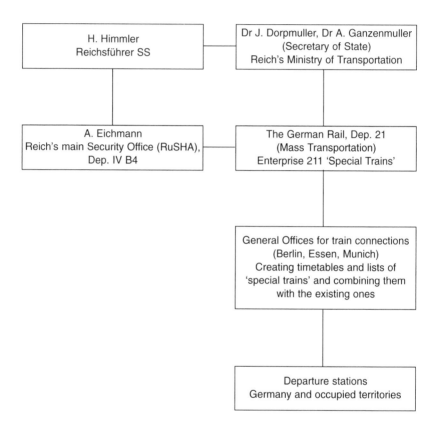

| H. Himmler Reichsführer SS | Dr J. Dorpmuller, Dr A. Ganzenmuller (Secretary of State) Reich's Ministry of Transportation |

| A. Eichmann Reich's main Security Office (RuSHA), Dep. IV B4 | The German Rail, Dep. 21 (Mass Transportation) Enterprise 211 'Special Trains' |

General Offices for train connections (Berlin, Essen, Munich) Creating timetables and lists of 'special trains' and combining them with the existing ones

Departure stations
Germany and occupied territories

Source: Burba, M. *Treblinka* (Lokheide, 1995), p. 16.

Appendix 6

SS Rank	US Army Equivalent	British Army Equivalent
Reichsführer	General of the Army	Field Marshal
SS-Oberstgruppenführer	General	General
SS-Obergruppenführer	Lieutenant-General	Lieutenant -General
SS-Gruppenführer	Major-General	Major-General
SS-Brigadeführer	Brigadier-General	Brigadier
SS-Oberführer	Senior Colonel	–
SS-Standartenführer	Colonel	Colonel
SS-Obersturmbannführer	Lieutenant-Colonel	Lieutenant-Colonel
SS-Sturmbannführer	Major	Major
SS-Hauptsturmführer	Captain	Captain
SS-Obersturmführer	First Lieutenant	Lieutenant
SS-Untersturmführer	Second Lieutenant	Second Lieutenant
SS-Sturmscharführer	Sergeant-Major	Regimental Sergeant-Major
SS-Stabsscharführer	Sergeant-Major	–
SS-Hauptscharführer	Master Sergeant	Sergeant-Major
SS-Oberscharführer	Technical Sergeant	Quartermaster Sergeant
SS-Scharführer	Staff Sergeant	Staff Sergeant
SS-Unterscharführer	Sergeant	Sergeant

APPENDIX 7
BELZEC EXTERMINATION CAMP*

Belzec's official name was SS-Sonderkommando Belzec, and it was also called 'Dienststelle Belzec der Waffen SS'. It was an extermination camp, the first of the three built for the purposes of Operation Reinhard. Construction began on 1 November 1941, and it was completed in February 1942. The first kommandant was Christian Wirth, who was superseded by Gottlieb Hering in August 1942. At the beginning of February 1942, experimental gassing of the Jews with bottled carbon monoxide was carried out. However, in the end, in a similar method to that used at the other camps, chambers using exhaust fumes from diesel engines were built in Belzec.

On 17 March 1942, the first transport of victims arrived at the camp. From that day until the middle of April, approximately 80,000 Jews were murdered. More than half of them were from Lublin and Lvov. Around 15 April there was a lull in the transports, which lasted a month. From the middle of May until the middle of June 1942, transports from Krakow and its vicinity were received at Belzec. There followed another month-long interval in the activity of the camp, this time caused by the need to enlarge the gas chambers. From the middle of July until the middle of December transports arrived regularly. During that period, 130,000 Jews from the Cracow district, 225,000 Jews from Lvov, approximately 300,000 Jews from the districts of Radom and Lublin, and several hundred Gypsies were murdered.

As was the case at Treblinka, specialized Jewish kommandos worked at the camp; they were later liquidated.

December 1942, was the turning point for Operation Reinhard. It marked the completion of the extermination of the majority of the Jews from the Government General. From that point on, fewer and fewer transports arrived at Belzec. During 'Operation 1005', carried out at the end of December 1942 and the beginning of January 1943, the mass graves of gassing victims were opened and the corpses were burnt. After the completion of the operation, the camp was liquidated by a group of 600 Jews who were subsequently sent to their deaths in Sobibor. Only a few Jews managed

---

* Source: Y. Arad, *Belzec, Sobibór, Treblinka: The Operation Reinhard Death Camps* (Bloomington, IN: Indiana University Press, 1999).

114

to escape from Belzec, and only one, Rudolf Reder, survived the war and wrote down his account.

APPENDIX 8
SOBIBOR EXTERMINATION CAMP*

Sobibor's official name was SS-Sonderkommando Sobibor, and it was the second of the extermination camps of Operation Reinhard. It was established in March 1942. The kommandants were, in turn, Richard Thomalla (responsible for the construction of the camp), Franz Stangl and Franz Reichsleitner.

The camp started to operate at the beginning of May 1942. From then until the end of July, approximately 90,000–100,000 Jews from the Lublin district, Czechoslovakia, Germany and Austria were murdered there. At the end of July 1942, transports ceased temporarily due to railroad works. At the end of August, work was started on expanding the number of gas chambers from three to six. During these construction works there was a change of kommandant at the camp; Stangl assumed the command of Treblinka, while Franz Reichsleitner came to Sobibor to replace him.

The camp resumed its activities at the beginning of October. Twenty-five thousand Jews from Slovakia were murdered during that month. In March 1943, 4,000 French Jews arrived in four transports, and between March and June, 35,000 Dutch Jews were brought to be killed. In the second half of February 1942, Himmler visited the camp to check on the efficiency of the corpse-burning operation.

Approximately 75,000 Jews from Lublin and the so-called 'West Galicia' district, and about 1,540,000 Jews from the Government General were killed in Sobibor in the period up to June 1943. The last transports (containing about 14,000 people) came from the ghettos in Vilnius, Minsk and Lida in September 1943. On 5 June 1943, on Himmler's order, the conversion of the extermination camp into a concentration camp was started. The uprising of the Jewish crew, on 14 October 1943, interrupted these works. As a consequence, it was decided to liquidate the camp; a process that lasted until the end of 1943. A small lodge was built on the grounds of the former camp in which one Ukrainian was installed, and the rest of site was levelled and planted with trees.

It is estimated that approximately 250,000 Jews and several hundred Poles and Gypsies were murdered in the death camp in Sobibor.

---

* Source: Arad, *Belzec, Sobibór, Treblinka*.

Bibliography

ARCHIVAL SOURCES

Archives of Düsseldorf's Court of 3 September 1965 – Judgement in the case of Kurt Franz.

Archives of Düsseldorf's Court of 22 December 1970 – Judgement in the case of Franz Stangl II-148 (1969 S-8 KS 1 (1969)).

Justiz und NS-Verbrechen. Saamlung deutscher strafurteile wegen nationalsozialistischer tötungsverbrechen 1945–1966 (University of Amsterdam, 1972).

Materialsammlung zu den Vernichtungslagern der Aktion Reinhard: Belzec, Sobibor, Treblinka (Bildungswerk Stanislaw Hantz e.V. 1995).

NS-Vernichtungslagern Belzec – Dokumenten sammlung (Bildungs-werk Stanislaw Hantz e.V. 1995).

Sobibor. Ein Vernichtungslagern im rahen der Aktion Reinhard (Bildungswerk Stanislaw Hantz e.V. 1995).

Summary in the case of death camp Treblinka, ZIH Archive, Warsaw.

The protocol of entry examination of the terrain of former death camp Treblinka, ZIH Archive, Warsaw.

Jurgen Stroop's report of the liquidation of the Warsaw ghetto, www.holocaust-history.org

Treblinka. Ein Vernichtungslager im rahen der Aktion Reinhard (Bildungswerk Stanislaw Hantz e.V. 1995).

Compilation of documents: *Eksterminacja Żydów na ziemiach polskich w okresie okupacji hitlerowskiej* (Warsaw 1957).

WEBSITES

Fritz Bauer Institut
www.fritz-bauer-institut.de

German Federal Archive
www.bundesarchive.de

Simon Wiesenthal's Center
www.wiesenthal.com

Museum of the Holocaust
www.ushmm.org

Yad Vashem Institute in Jerusalem
www.yad-vashem.org.il

Compilation of documents made by young historians
www.holocaust-history.org

The Holocaust Chronicle – an e-book. Compilation of knowledge
about the Holocaust
www.holocaustchronicle.org

Compilation of present pictures from sites of former death camps
www.imagesforreflection.com

Databases for people who lost their families during the Holocaust
www.jewishgen.org/registry
www. holocaustnames.com

Site about camps of Operation Reinhard and more
www.jewishgen.org/forgottencamps

The Nizkor Project – Ken McVay's site: one of the first sites about
the extermination of Jews during World War Two
www.nizkor.org

Chronology of the extermination of Jews in Europe
www.historyplace.com/worldwar2/holocaust/timeline.html

Site in the German language: offers much interesting information
and is frequently updated
www.shoahproject.org

BIBLIOGRAPHY SOURCES

Bartoszewski, W., 'Martyrologia Polski 1939–45 w pamietnikach i dokumentach', *Poradnik Bibliotekarza*, 139 (1961), 10.

Bibliography of Books in Hebrew on Jewish Catastrophe and Heroism in Europe (Yad Vashem, 1960).

Bloomberg, M., *The Holocaust: An Annotated Bibliography and Resource Guide* (San Bernardino, CA/New York, 1985).

Bukowska, M. and Wysocka, M., *Wykaz zespolow i zbiorow przechowywanych w Archiwum GKBZHwP/1978* (Warsaw: Ministerstwo Sprawiedliwosci, 1978).

Cargas, J., *The Holocaust: Annotated Bibliography* (Hereford Catholic Library Association, 1977).

Catalogue of Camps and Prisons in Germany and German-Occupied Territories (Arlosen: ITS, Rewards, 1949).

Chojnacki, W., Pospieszalski, M. and Serwanski, E., *Materialy do bibliografii okupacji hitlerowskiej w Polsce 1939–45: Uzupelnienie za lata 1944–53* (Warsaw: PWN, 1957).

Duraczyński, E., *Wydawnictwo Yad Vashem: Dzieje najnowsze*, Vol. 2 (1969).

Edelheit, A.J., *Bibliography of Holocaust Literature* (Boulder, CO: 1986 [up to 1985]).

Kiedyńska, W., *Zestawienie międzynarodowej literatury o hitlerowskich obozach koncentracyjnych* (Warsaw, 1950).

Kania, S., *Publikacje GKBZHwP 1945–1982* (Warsaw, 1983).

Kosicki, J., *Bibliografia pismiennictwa polskiego w latach 1944–53 o hitlerowskich zbrodniach wojennych* (Warsaw: Wydawnictwo Prawnicze, 1955).

Lasha, V., *Nazism, Resistance and Holocaust in World War II: A Bibliography* (Metuchen, NJ: Scarecrow Press Inc., 1985).

Mark, B., *Meczenstwo i walka Zydow w latach okupacji. Poradnik bibliograficzny* (Warsaw: Biblioteka Narodowa, 1963).

Sable, M.H., *Holocaust Studies Directory and Bibliography of Bibliographies* (Westport, CT: Greenwood, 1987).
The Ghetto Anthology: Comprehensive Chronicle of the Extermination of Jewry (Los Angeles, CA: 1985).
The Holocaust in Books and Films: A List (New York: International Center for Holocaust Studies, 1986).
Zbrodnie hitlerowskie na dzieciach i mlodziezy polskiej 1939–45 (Warsaw, 1969).

REFERENCES

Arad, Y., *Documents of the Holocaust* (Jerusalem: Yad Vashem, 1981).
Arad, Y., *Bełżec, Sobibór, Treblinka: The Operation Reinhard Death Camps* (Bloomington, IN: Indiana University Press, 1999).
Aarons, M. and Loftus, J., *Akcja Ocalenie: watykanska przystan nazistow* (Warsaw: Alma-Press, 1994).
Bednarz, W., *Oboz stracen w Chelmnie nad Nerem* (Warsaw: GKBZH, 1946).
Benz, W. (ed.), *History of Nazi Concentration Camps: Studies, Reports, Documents* (Dachau: Barbara Distel, 1994).
Berenstein, T. and Rutkowski, A., 'Hitlerowskie sprawozdanie statystyczne o zagladzie Zydów w Europie', *Biuletyn Żydowskiego Instytuto Historycznego*, 6 (1968), pp. 79–83.
Biblia Tysiaclecia [*The Bible*]
Blatt, T., *Sobibor: The Forgotten Revolt* (Seattle: Holocaust Education Center, 1998).
Blatt, T., *Nur die Schatten bleiben: Aufstand im Vernichtungslager Sobibor* (Berlin, Aufbau: Verl., 2000).
Browning, Ch., *Zwykli ludzie: 101 Policyjny Batalion Rezerwy i 'Ostateczne Rozwiazanie' w Polsce* (Warsaw: Bellona, 2000).
Bryja, M. and Ledwoch, J., *Jednostki Waffen SS 1939–1945* (Warsaw: Militaria, 1996).
Burba, M., *Treblinka* (Lokheide, 1995).
Cohen, E.A., *De Negentien trainen naar Sobibor* (Amsterdam: Elsevier, 1989).
Czarkowski, R., *Cieniom Treblinki* (Warsaw: Wydawnictwo MON, 1989).
Das Meschenschlachthaus Treblinka, Vol. 2 (Wien, 1946).
de Mildt, D., *The Euthanasia and Aktion Reinhard Trial Cases: In the*

Name of the People: Perpetrators of Genocide in the Reflection of Their Post War Prosecution in the West (The Hague: Martinus Nijhoff Publishers, 1999).

Donat, A., *Death Camp Treblinka: Documentation* (New York: Holocaust Library, 1979).

Eisenbach, A., *Hitlerowska polityka zaglady Zydow* (Warsaw: Ksiazka i Wiedza, 1961).

Von Hanno, L. and Winter, B., *NS-Euthanasie vor Gericht: Fritz Bauer und die Grenzen juristischer Bewaltingung* (Frankfurt-am-Main: campus Verl., 1996).

Glazar, R., *Trap with a Green Fence* (Northwestern University Press, 1995).

Głowna Komisja Badania Zbrodni Hitlerowskich w Polsce: Obozy hitlerowskie na ziemiach polskich 1939–1945. Informator encyklopedyczny (Warsaw, 1979).

Grodzinski, E., *Filozofia Adolfa Hitlera w Mein Kampf* (Warsaw/ Olsztyn: Wydawnictwo Ethos, 1992).

Grosman, W., *Pieklo Treblinki* (Katowice: Wydawnictwo Literatura Polska, 1945).

Grünberg, K., *Biografia Hitlera* (Warsaw: Ksiażka i Wiedza, 1989).

Grünberg, K., *SS-Gwardia Hitlera* (Warsaw: Ksiażka i Wiedza, 1994).

Gulczynski, J., *Oboz smierci w Chelmnie nad Nerem* (Konin: Muzeum Okregowe, 1991).

Gumkowski, J., *Treblinka: teksty historyczne* (Warsaw: Rada Obrony Pomnikow Walki i Meczenstwa, 1962).

Gumkowski, J. and Kulakowski, T., *Zbrodniarze Hitlerowscy przed Najwyzszym Trybunalem Narodowym* (Warsaw: Wydawnictwo Prawnicze, 1967).

Heydecker, J. and Leeb, J., *Trzecia Rzesza w swietle Norymbergi- bilans tysiaca lat* (Warsaw: Ksiażka i Wiedza, 1979).

Höss, R., *Autobiografia* (Warsaw: Wydawnictwo Prawnicze, 1989).

Klee, E., Dressen, W. and Riess, V., *The Good Old Days* (New York: The Free Press, 1988).

Kogon, E., *Nationalistiche Massentotungen durch Giftgas* (Frankfurt-am-Main, 1983).

Kriger, E., *Niemiecka fabryka smierci w Lublinie* (Moskwa: Wydawnictwo Literatury Jezyków Obcych, 1944).

Krolikowski, J., 'Budowałem most kolejowy w pobliżu Treblinki', *Biuletyn Żydowskiego Instytuto Historycznego*, 49 (1964), pp. 45–62.

Krzepicki, A., '18 dni w Treblince', *Biuletyn Żydowskiego Instytuto Historycznego*, 43/44 (1962), pp. 85–109.

Kuperhand, M., *Shadows of Treblinka* (Chicago, IL: University of Illinois, 1998).

Leszczynski, J., 'Od formuly obozu zaglady – Höppner–Chelmno n/Nerem – do Endlösung', *Biuletyn Żydowskiego Instytuto Historycznego*, 4 (1978), pp. 40–55.

Leszczynski, K., 'Eksterminacja ludności na ziemiach polskich 1939–1945', *Biuletyn Głównej Komisji Badania Zbrodni Hitlerowskich w Polsce*, 11 (1960), pp. 30–78.

Lord Russell of Liverpool, *Pod biczem swastyki* (Warsaw: Czytelnik, 1956).

Lord Russell of Liverpool, *Proces Eichmanna* [*Eichmann's Trial*] (Warsaw: Czytelnik, 1966).

Łukaszewicz, Z., *Oboz zaglady Treblinka* (Warsaw: PIW, 1946).

Majewski, R., *Waffen SS: Mity i rzeczywistosc* (Wroclaw: Krajowa Agencja Wydawnicza, 1983).

Manvell, R. and Fraenkel, H., *H. Himmler* (Warsaw, 1972).

Marczewska, K., 'Treblinka w swietle akt delegatury rzadu RP na kraj', *Biuletyn Głównej Komisji Badania Zbrodni Hitlerowskich w Polsce*, 19 (1968), pp. 50–94.

Marszalek, J., *Obozy pracy w Generalnym Gubernatorstwie w latach 1939–1945* (Lublin: Państwowe Muzeum na Majdanku, 1998).

Materials from session, *Osrodek zaglady w Chelmnie nad Nerem i jego rola w hitlerowskiej polityce eksterminacyjnej* (Konin: Muzeum Okregowe, 1995).

May, H., 'Niemiecki nadlesniczy o zagladzie Zydów w Chelmnie nad Nerem', *Przeglad Zachodni*, 3 (1962), pp. 5–9.

Mendelsohn, E., *Zydzi Europy srodkowo-wschodniej w okresie miedzywojennym* (Warsaw: PWN, 1992).

Mikulski, J., *Medycyna hitlerowska w sluzbie III Rzeszy* (Warsaw: PWN, 1981).

Mitschelich, A. and Mielke, F., *Nieludzka medycyna* (Warsaw: Panstwowy Zaklad Wydawnictw Lekarskich, 1963).

Novitch, M., *Sobibor: Martyrdom and Revolt* (New York: Holocaust Library, 1980).

Padfield, P., *Himmler: Reichsführer SS* (Warsaw: Interart, 1997).

Piotrowski, S., *Misja Odyla Globocnika: sprawozdanie o wynikach finansowych zaglady Zydów w Polsce* (Warsaw: PIW, 1949).

Piotrowski, S., *Dziennik Hansa Franka* (Warsaw: Wydawnictwo Prawnicze, 1956).

Rajgrodski, J., 'Jedenascie miesiecy w obozie zaglady w Treblince', *Biuletyn Żydowskiego Instytutu Historycznego*, 25 (1958), pp. 59–79.

Ramme, A., *Sluzba bezpieczenstwa SS* (Warsaw: Wydawnictwo MON, 1975).

Raschke, R., *Escape from Sobibor* (Chicago, IL: University of Illinois Press, 1995).

Reder, R., *Belzec* (Krakow, 1946).

Ringelblum, E., *Kronika getta warszawskiego* (Warsaw: Czytelnik, 1983).

Ruckerl, A., *NS-Vernichtungslager im Spiegel deutscher Stadtprozzesse* (München, 1977).

Sawicki, J., *Przed polskim prokuratorem: dokumenty i komentarze* (Warsaw: Iskry, 1961).

Schlevis, J., *Vernichtungslager Sobibor* (Berlin: Metropol, 1998).

Sereny, G., *Into that Darkness: From Mercy Killing to Mass Murder* (London: Penguin, 1998).

Serwański, E., *Oboz zaglady w Chelmnie nad Nerem* (Poznan, 1964).

Steiner, J.F., *Treblinka* (Meridian Books, 2000).

Szmajzer, S., *Hell in Sobibor* (Brasilia, 1979).

Torzecki, R., *Polacy i Ukraincy: sprawa ukrainska w czasie II wojny swiatowej na terenie II Rzeczypospolitej* (Warsaw: PWN, 1993).

Tregenza, M., 'Christian Wirth a pierwsza faza Akcji Reinhard', *Zeszyty Majdanka*, Vol. 14 (Lublin: Panstwowe Muzeum na Majdanku, 1992) .

Wiernik, J., *Rok w Treblince* (Warsaw: Komisja Koordynacyjna, 1944).

Willenberg, S., *Bunt w Treblince* (Warsaw: Res Publica, 1991).

Wilczur, J., *Scigalem Iwana Groznego* (Wydawnictwo Ethos, 1993).

Wojtczak, S., 'Karny oboz pracy Treblinka I i osrodek zaglady Treblinka II', *Biuletyn Głównej Komisji Badania Zbrodni Hitlerowskich w Polsce*, 26, 29 (1975), pp. 36–97.

Zabecki, F., *Wspomnienia dawne i nowe* (Warsaw: PAX, 1977).